# Charter Schools
## and the
# Corporate Makeover
## of
# Public Education

WHAT'S AT STAKE?

# Charter Schools
## and the
# Corporate Makeover
## of
# Public Education

### WHAT'S AT STAKE?

**Michael Fabricant**
**Michelle Fine**
*Foreword by Deborah Meier*

Teachers College, Columbia University
New York and London

Published by Teachers College Press, 1234 Amsterdam Avenue, New York, NY 10027

*Library of Congress Cataloging-in-Publication Data*

Fabricant, Michael.
Charter schools and the corporate makeover of public education : what's at stake? / Michael Fabricant, Michelle Fine ; foreword by Debbie Meier.
    p. cm.
 Includes bibliographical references and index.
 ISBN 978-0-8077-5285-2 (pbk.)
  1.  Charter schools—United States. 2.  Business and education—United States. 3.  Education—Economic aspects—United States. 4.  Educaion—Aims and objectives—United States. I. Fine, Michelle. II. Title.
  LB2806.36.F34 2012
  371.050973—dc23
                                                              2011031855
 ISBN 978-0-8077-5285-2 (paper)

Printed                          on                    acid-free                    paper
Manufactured in the United States of America

19   18   17   16   15   14   13   12          8   7   6   5   4   3   2   1

To Joan Driscoll Kelly, who died far too young but left a powerful legacy for the housing/homelessness movement and, more generally, as a peaceful warrior for social justice.

To Maxine Greene, who stretches our educational imagination toward justice, inquiry, laughter, and action, engaging educators to imagine what could be even as we struggle through what is.

And, of course, to educators, parents, and students engaged in struggles across the country to save the precious, delicate, deeply flawed public in public education.

# Contents

FOREWORD *by Deborah Meier*                                          ix

ACKNOWLEDGMENTS                                                      xiii

1. AN INTRODUCTION TO THE LANDSCAPE
   OF CHARTER REFORM                                                 1
   The Rise of the Charter School Movement                          2
   Charter Schools, Public Education,
       and the Front Line of a Contested Political Terrain          5
   Charters in the History of Educational Choice                    7
   What Is at Stake?                                                 8
   The Structure of the Book                                        9

2. THE PROMISE: THE GENESIS OF EXPECTATION
   AND THE CHALLENGE OF CHARTER REFORM                              12
   The Luster and Contribution of Exemplar Charter Schools          14
   A History of Charters in Three Movements                         17
   The Policy Landscape: Commitments and Variation                  21
   The Charter Landscape                                            21
   Policy Dimensions: Are Charter Schools Public Institutions?      23
   Charters, the Marketplace, and a Theory of Change                26
   The Appeal of Charters to Dominant Economic Interests:
       Monetizing Public Education                                  27
   The Question of Money and Corruption                             31
   Scaling up Reform Through a Network of Charters:
       The Tradeoffs of Efficiency—and Economic Advantage           32
   Parents' Search for Alternatives to a System That Has Disinvested  33

3. THE TENSION BETWEEN PROMISE AND EVIDENCE                         37
   The Promise-Evidence Gap                                         37
   Charters and the Promise of Equity                               45
   Charter School Dropouts, Pushouts, and Graduation Rates:
       Why Do We Know So Little?                                    48
   The Effect of Charters on Parent Involvement                     52
   The Promise of Charter Innovation as a Pathway
       to Improving Public Education                                54

Teacher Experience and Stability as Predicates for Innovation            58
Summary                                                                  59

4.  INTERLOCKING POWER AND THE DEREGULATION
    OF PUBLIC EDUCATION                                                   61
    The Influence of Wealth on Public Policy                             62
    The State and Philanthropy                                           63
    The Charter Campaign and Political Mobilization of the Private Sector:
        The Case of New York State                                       66
    Charter Schools and the Maximization of Economic Gain:
        Profiting from the Privatization of Public Schools               68
    The Slippery Question of Profit and the Consolidation of Power       69
    Partnership and Profit in the Game of Educational Privatization      75
    Claiming Market Share:
        Strategic Organizing of the Charter Campaign                     77
    Collateral Damage: The Loss of Accountability                        85
    Reflections on Politics, Economics, and Ideology                     86

5.  "CRISIS": A MOMENT FOR DISPOSSESSION AND PROFIT                       88
    In a Landscape of Inequality: Whose Crisis Is It Anyway?             90
    After the Floods: Charter Growth in New Orleans                      91
    Building an Education Renaissance:
        Chicago and Charter Education                                    95
    Declaring "Crisis":
        School Closings and Charter Openings in New York City            98
    A Geography and Archeology of Dispossession:
        Tracking the Policies and Their Impact                           100
    Making a Science of Dispossession:
        Focus on Testing, Ignore Dropout                                 102
    The Dropout Epidemic                                                 104
    Conclusion                                                           106

6.  RECLAIMING "PUBLIC": DEEPENING NATIONAL COMMITMENTS
    TO PUBLIC INVESTMENT AND PUBLIC INNOVATION                           108
    New Jersey: The Budget Crisis and Public Education                   108
    The Binary Tradeoffs of Charter Policy                               111
    Provocative Images of Public Innovation                              115
    Toward a New Consensus: The Increasing Call for Investment
        to Spur Innovation and Foster Effective Schooling                117
    Reimagining and Reinvesting in a Public Education                    126
    Conclusion                                                           130

REFERENCES                                                               131

INDEX                                                                    143

ABOUT THE AUTHORS                                                        153

# Foreword

"What we consider 'public' in the United States is under construction. . . . Our commitment to shared fates, democratic participation, and concerns for equity... are in jeopardy." So begins this careful and important book on the meaning of the current charter movement in education. At the heart of the challenge facing us are the contradictions and dilemmas inherent in the idea of the public, the republic, and democracy itself. Thus, the "one best way" to connect schools to the people is not simple, obvious, or inevitable.

We are witnessing a strategic redefinition of democracy in which the free marketplace of goods and services is not merely a necessary prerequisite, but represented as the highest form of democracy. Currently, the view of many on the Right is that anything interfering with such corporate freedom is a step toward dictatorship. The dilemma of democracy, justice, and how to successfully educate children of poverty underlies Michelle Fine and Michael Fabricant's efforts to pull apart the arguments for and against what is now called "the charter school movement." This volume lifts up for critical analysis how public schools have in the past, and must again, attach to a democratic vision. The authors provide substantial evidence of how the charter school movement has been corralled away from democracy and toward privatization of public education. Additionally, this book invites a much-needed discussion on how to restore public education to a place where decisions are made close to home by educators, parents, communities, and youth, where accountability runs both deep and participatory through the democratic examination of a wide range of evidence, and where Dewey's notion of education as a critical capillary of democracy flourishes.

In light of the privatizing zeal to "save" public schools, I have had opportunity for reflection upon whether some of my earlier work may have inadvertently carved a path toward what we now witness. Like Michelle Fine, I was deeply involved in the small schools movement, which may now be seen as the forerunner of today's charter schooling. We thought that a series of small schools, democratically designed by educators for and with communities, would produce better schools than those designed and implemented from a distance by way of bureaucratic rules and regulations, and where teachers were interchangeable parts of a single-minded curriculum and pedagogy. We believed that if we built schools rooted in a vision of education where communities, parents, teachers, and students could learn together from their experiences, we might produce schools that better educated all Americans. For this purpose we argued that schools needed to be smaller than most American schools were becoming, so that more direct forms of discourse (e.g., face-to-face) could take place. We learned from districts such as East Harlem in New York City where, under a system of partial community control, 21 buildings serving a K–8 student population were transformed into 52 schools—half intended as neighborhood zoned schools, and the other half as schools of choice. The idea caught on and began to spread to district after district as teachers and parents got excited by the idea of starting their own schools; local school boards in New York City saw this as an opportunity to maintain a healthy student population and perhaps even increase their numbers. We argued that these small, innovative schools should accept all students but bureaucratically be relatively autonomous—that is, we were coupling autonomy, equity, and democracy. Now we see this braid has come undone. "Reformers" in the charter school movement fight for autonomy, but not equity or democracy.

By the early 1990s the small schools movement in New York City encompassed several dozen schools serving over 25,000 students and nationwide was growing daily. We transformed a few major high school buildings into smaller schools of choice, and we developed a proposal for creating a larger zone for 50,000 students, where school teachers, administrators, and communities—with the support of two major universities, the teacher's union, the local board of education, and even Superintendent of the State of New York—might create a 5-year experiment in greater autonomy and new forms of accountability. When such explorations were stalled, many of us supported charter schools that were not part of such local management/labor agreements, and that had their own privately selected boards with both public and private funding sources.

When charters were part of a movement for democratic schooling we saw them as providing an opportunity to explore new ideas and persuade the larger public and profession of alternatives to the existing public schools. As small schools began to traffic with charter schools, we reminded our colleagues of John Dewey's belief that education for democracy cannot separate its curricular purposes from its pedagogical practices and from the relationship that people within such schools have with each other. We prevailed on the issue of "small," but democracy in schools—with communities, by educators, for critical dissent and inquiry—got lost in the mix. Schooling for ruling survived as privatization corrupted the small schools movements. This is the historic turn that Fabricant and Fine delineate.

Everyone wants college graduates who think critically and participate actively in civic life. But what is not being pursued in the contemporary discussion of "education reform" is how such rhetoric connects with democracy in a society of growing inequality gaps. We're too busy passing laws, new regulations, deadlines, and test-score goals to ask penetrating questions about how any of this will strengthen our multiracial democracy; how can we keep buying into a simplistic theory that higher test scores will, by any means, produce a stronger economy? In short, we need the space and time for the educational, political, and ethical innovation that charters may once have heralded—"mom and pop" small schools and charters started by dedicated and curious parents and teachers who had interesting ideas, committed themselves to accepting all children, were open and transparent in their practices, and would track their graduates 2–8 years later for feedback on the school's impact on their lives. Fabricant and Fine suggest that schooling is fast becoming something quite different—a publicly subsidized system of privately controlled franchises to replace what the Right frequently calls "political monopolies": in other words, our existing schools. We must create criteria for what evidence we will collect and provide publicly supported venues for describing these schools and their outcomes in communities all over the nation. In addition, we need ways to get simple, reliable data on attendance, dropouts, pushouts, test scores, and so forth, which means data with no high stakes attached: The higher the stakes, the more questionable the data. If we can use the aforementioned time and space to persuade and be persuaded by our allies and some of our current opponents, we might go back to that moment a decade or more ago when so many optimistically believed that public schools could be a way to strengthen the knowledge, the values, and the habits of mind and heart that democracy rests upon.

To be clear, we must reject niche schools for a particular social class, race, or ethnicity that possess restrictive assumptions about our common humanity. Nor can we hold any school to the unrealistic task of solving the problems that inequities in income and wealth produce, especially at a time when such inequities are growing dramatically worse. But we can perhaps develop young people better prepared to understand, contest, and tackle such issues. We can do this by working within the framework of existing public structures and accepting as a default the argument that decisions should be made close to the family and the child, the teacher and the school.

Michael Fabricant and Michelle Fine's book is an ideal starting point for these kinds of discussions. They lay out sufficient evidence and a range of potential directions based on respect for what evidence we have and what evidence we still lack. While they clearly have a point of view that they do not hide, they lay the groundwork for opening the door for democratic debate before we reach the point of no return. Jefferson's dream—expanded to include all the people—has yet to be truly been tried out. Now is the time to accept the challenge of educating all—alongside our young people, our colleagues, our fellow citizens, and ourselves.

*—Deborah Meier*

# Acknowledgments

In the development of this book we have been the beneficiaries of many colleagues' kindnesses and their substantial expertise regarding this perilous moment for democratic public education. Stan Karp, Leo Casey, and Leigh Dingerson provided especially helpful commentary on a late draft of the manuscript. Their sharp insights and imagination resulted in a number of modifications. Equally important, reviews by Steve Burghardt, Nicole Fabricant, Sam Finesurrey, and Eric Zachary of parts of the book helped us to more thoughtfully contextualize the work. Sam Coleman, Edwin Mayorga, Charles Payne, Maddy Fox, Brett Stoudt, Lauren Wells, Barbara Reisman, Danielle Farrie, and many others helped us move through the affective, emotional, and political tumult, so that we might comfortably distinguish an appreciation for some exemplary charter schools and still a deep skepticism about the charter social movement for privatization. We thank W. E. B. Du Bois for holding us accountable to the real, historic "crisis" that is America.

As well, Carole Saltz and Emily Renwick of Teachers College Press carefully reviewed the manuscript and offered a number of important recommendations. For example, they posed a series of incisive questions about both the meaning of a public institution in the 21st century and the impact of the charter school movement on public policy, which helped us to rethink parts of the analysis. Alana Glaser was especially helpful in highlighting formatting, editing, and substantive issues in a very last stage of manuscript preparation, and Kendra Urdang and Jared Becker helped us to assemble, organize, and locate parts of the bibliography.

Our acknowledgments would not be complete without a shoutout to our partners Betsy Fabricant and David Surrey, who attentively listened as we conveyed our excitement about the project; offered important feedback during crucial moments of its development; and, most importantly, believed in the importance of this work even as our faith on occasion faltered. We hope the contributions of colleagues, friends, and family are rewarded through the substance and impact of the book's argument. Finally, this obligatory and necessary caveat must be offered: although the contributions of others were critical to the refinement and development of this work, responsibility for its content is ours alone.

# CHAPTER 1

# An Introduction to the Landscape of Charter Reform

As we write, and then as you read, what we consider "public" in the United States is under construction. This radical renovation of the public sector, designed and paid for by private philanthropy, corporate politics, and the federal government, bears dramatic consequences for restructuring class, race/ethnic arrangements, and the future of public institutions. Public resources, governance, responsibility, opportunities, and aspirations are being redistributed. Significant institutions that bind our communities—public housing, welfare, libraries, senior centers, and education—are on the receiving end of unprecedented budget cuts, sustained disinvestment, and vitriolic attack. At this historic moment of watershed change, our national commitments to shared fates, democratic participation, concerns for equity, and deep accountability are in jeopardy: increasingly understood as a sweet thread of nostalgia. More significantly, the membrane between public and private is leaking badly. Perhaps it always has, but the seepage has breached the levees, so to speak, of public spaces. The role of business in state affairs is assumed to be essential, while the participation of community members as stakeholders seems passé.

At this juncture in the history of public education, Democrats and Republicans have found a troubling space to agree in ushering in the "new normal" of disinvestment in poor communities of color and the upward redistribution of tax breaks for the rich. Prisons and the military engorge and have become the most expansive sector of the state, and corporate thinking and policies encroach on government. We find ourselves worrying about the future of democracy, equity, and accountability and the erosion of the "public" in public education.

We have seen these reconfigurations before, in housing, health care, and in the debates over welfare/workfare, the privatization of prisons, the defunding of low-income housing. But the pace and radical makeover of the public sector in this moment is unprecedented and deserve close analysis—to pause and parse the layered social forces of politics, ideologies, media coverage, and economics and the consequences of this power-ful convergence on the ground, especially in poor communities of color.

## THE RISE OF THE CHARTER SCHOOL MOVEMENT

In this book, we investigate through the prism of the rapid ascension of the charter school movement the strategic remaking of the public sector. We believe that the rise of charters as a new public-education option—an ambiguous, hybrid education form originated by labor and social justice educators but marketed now by a well-funded campaign as *the* answer to class and race opportunity gaps—is an especially vivid and compelling reform lens through which to dissect the disturbing, complex, and com-peting ideologies, economics, political motives, and community desires reshaping the public sector.

Throughout this volume we distinguish between individual char-ter schools and the charter school movement—interrogating the space between promise and evidence—analyzing through a lens of critical race-and-class analysis who is making money, whose power is being re-consolidated, and who pays the heaviest price for our national makeover.

A history in brief:

Charters, after all, were developed in the 1980s by progressive educa-tors under the stewardship of Albert Shanker and the American Federa-tion of Teachers. Teachers sought to create small, engaging educational settings within low-income communities, where children of poverty, of color, and immigrants could be educated well, cared for, and nurtured academically with intent. In the beginning, charters dotted the education-al landscape as an educational alternative. There soon came a moment, however, when the social justice motor was appropriated and reengi-neered by philanthropic, corporate, hedge-fund and real estate interests. While the charters of the 1980s were largely educator run and commu-nity rooted, the charters of today have been catapulted into a corporate movement associated with a relentless attack on teachers and teacher unions, the ideological critique of public education as in "crisis," and con-sequent seductive advertisements for families to exit the public sector.

Indeed, there has been a public opinion and media campaign launched. The campaign, although penetrating the consciousness of the electorate, nourishes a profound contradiction. If charters educate only a small fraction of children in the United States, how is it possible that adults who read the newspaper, listen to radio, or watch television see charters as a primary if not *the* primary answer to what ails public educa-tion? More to the point, according to the PDK/Gallup Poll of 2010:

> Americans increasingly embrace public charter schools. Sixty-eight percent of Americans have a favorable opinion of charter schools, and almost two out of three Americans would support a new public charter school in their communities. Sixty percent of Americans say they would support a large increase in the number of public charter schools operating in the United States. (*Phi Delta Kappan*, 2010, October)

The contemporary charter movement has deployed and consolidated financial, cultural, media, and political resources to sell charters to Americans as a wedge institution to marginalize and shrink the old public sector and announce the formation of the new. It is the most vivid institutional expression to date of the changing of the political guard from liberal New Dealers to centrist/right New Democrats and far right Republicans. These profound political tremors have erupted consistently over the past 30 years, leaving in their wake scarring policy markers of privatization, corporatization, and the deregulation of public institutions. The charter movement, however, reflects an especially brash institutional expression of a diminished political aspiration to create a public sector underpinned by democratic participation, strategic investment based on empirical evidence, development of a skilled professional workforce, comprehensive accountability to a larger public, and equitable investment across class as well as race.

Individual charter schools are considered part of the public school landscape; indeed, most of their fiscal base derives from tax-levy dollars. And yet it is curious that the charter campaign, embodied in organizations like Democrats for Education Reform, films like *Waiting for Superman*, and proclamations from governors like Chris Christie in New Jersey, has been explicitly and relentlessly dedicated to wholesale critique of the public education system, fingering the presumed incompetence of teachers who work within the system and the unions that have been at the heart of urban schooling as singularly culpable for its problems. There is, however, a growing resistance movement.

For example, in July 2010, a coalition of civil rights organizations submitted the "Framework for Providing All Students an Opportunity to Learn through Reauthorization of the Elementary and Secondary Education Act," a bold statement for equitable opportunities to learn, a sharp critique of Race to the Top, and a soft caution about the federal push for charters.

> We have reservations about the extensive reliance on charter schools in the Blueprint's turnaround strategies. While charters can serve as laboratories for innovation . . . there must also be safeguards to ensure that charter schools

do not promote education-driven gentrification through the disproportionate exclusion of students with the greatest needs. (Lawyers Committee for Civil Rights Under Law et al., 2010, July, 9–10)

In this book we track the history of charters from social justice alternatives to a campaign to dismantle and decentralize public education, through to the contemporary movements for educational justice. It is within this context that the following six questions animate our writing:

- How did a social justice education movement, initiated by teachers and teachers' unions, evolve into a corporate campaign to dismantle existing structures of public education?
- What is the relationship between the promise of charters and contemporary evidence of their impact?
- Even if charters in the aggregate were academically more successful than local schools—and the evidence is dubious—what are the consequences of a deregulated charter movement for participatory democracy, racial equity, and deep accountability to community and youth?
- How does the twinning of corporate profit and Black/Latino/poor community pain manifest itself in the current rush to reshape public institutions toward private interests and ever more inequitable forms of (dis)investment?
- Recognizing that charters are now here to stay on the public education landscape, what safeguards need to be put into place to ensure that these schools remain public, democratic, accessible to all, and deeply accountable?
- Given the well-documented and racialized/class-based troubles of public education and the dramatic impact of systematic, cumulative, miseducation in low-income communities of color, what are the elements of public innovation and strategic investment that can promote educational justice?

*Charter Schools and the Corporate Makeover of Public Education* is written to explore these questions about contemporary conditions in public education through the lens of the charter-school movement. We frame the text by taking into account the commitment of a small group of exemplary charter schools dedicated to social justice, as well as the well-funded private sector and federal campaign to sell charters as *the* market answer to public education and the cumulative record of disappointment of public education in low-income communities of color.

Importantly, this book is neither anti-charter nor an apology for the dismal aggregate state of public education in low-income communities. Indeed, we have great respect for those educators, parents, youth, and community leaders who have struggled to create spaces where young people otherwise denied quality education can be respected, engaged, and educated. Both of us have written on the deep and scarring inequities that litter the landscape of public education. We are, however, intensely suspect of the well-funded charter campaign that sells the American public on the idea that "chartering" a very small slice of public education while cutting strategic investment in the larger whole project of education will make our schools more effective.

We write with worries about four fading American values: public education as foundational to civic *participation* and *democracy*; schools with *strong accountability* to youth, parents, and community; *sustainability* of educational communities over time; and the *equitable distribution* of resources and opportunities for all children. We recognize that these values have never been fully enacted in the history of U.S. education but worry that they are now being abandoned.

The charter movement has emerged at a moment in history when educational despair inside communities of color runs high, ideological calls for privatization have gained prominence, unions are under siege, accountability regimes have been mobilized to declare public schools a site of crisis, and all that is public is being hotly contested. We, as educators and parents, understand why parents, especially those in under-invested communities, where so much of public education has failed their children for generations, would seek a voucher, enroll in a charter, and yearn for an alternative to provide a better life for their children. At the same time, as social analysts, we are witnessing the restructuring of public education and, therefore, must ask a series of questions about the experience of charter reform. Who is being gentrified out of the charter revolution? Are charters indeed the source of innovation that the federal government declares? What is their record? Who's making money?

## CHARTER SCHOOLS, PUBLIC EDUCATION, AND THE FRONT LINE OF A CONTESTED POLITICAL TERRAIN

Of all the civil rights for which the world has struggled and fought for 5,000 years, the right to learn is undoubtedly the most fundamental. The freedom to learn, curtailed even as it is today, has been bought by bitter sacrifice. And whatever we may think of the curtailment of other civil rights we should fight to the last ditch to keep open the right to learn, the right to examine in our schools not only what we believe but

what we do not believe, not only what our leaders say . . . We must
insist upon this to give our children the fairness of a start which will
equip them with such an array of facts and such an attitude toward truth
that they can have a real chance to judge what the world is and what
its greater minds have thought it might be. (W. E. B. Du Bois,1970, pp.
230–231)

In the midst of the McCarthy era, W. E. B. Du Bois defended as essential
the contentious, ever flawed, yet intimate relation of democracy and public education. As he notes in this essay, the project of public education in
the United States has had a long and checkered history. The goals have
always been contested.

For many, schools have been, primarily, a mechanism for socializ-
ing and sorting a stratified workforce, capable of meeting the economic
demands of a particular era, reproducing the very race, class, and gender divisions that organize our political economy. For others, schools
promote upward mobility through the equitable distribution of public
resources to school systems, no matter the race and income of the student body. But a third stream of thought, articulated by Du Bois and
many since, is that education should be fundamental to democracy and
to the project of racial justice and reducing inequality. This perspective
is steeped in an understanding of public schools as a collective space
where youth, educators, and their families are supported to think hard,
inquire, play, explore, learn about what is, and imagine what could be
and to act on the world as engaged citizens. In the company of perhaps
libraries, parks, juries, and public transit, public schools are one of the
few places where we as a nation mingle across race/ethnic lines and
zip codes; a system upon which we are all dependent for growth and
development; the basis of our collective present and future; the institution that can ignite knowledge, dissent, and community. Importantly,
in the United States, public schools have never successfully fulfilled this
vision, particularly in poor communities, immigrant communities, and
communities of color. And yet public schools remain perhaps the most
critical site of struggle for achieving some part of this iconic dream of
American citizenship.

Perhaps most fundamentally, education as a public good is being de-
stabilized. If ever there was an American Dream, public education was
invented to promote its actualization. Even wise skeptics like Du Bois
recognize this potential. But today both the American dream and its
essential invention, public education, are threatened with radical transformation.

## CHARTERS IN THE HISTORY OF EDUCATIONAL CHOICE

Over time, the charter movement has become a multi-threaded fabric, with strands of social justice educators, parents looking for viable alternatives to failing local schools, desperate communities suddenly swept up by the neoliberal winds of privatizing interests, profits, and an anti-union, anti-government agenda. A confusing swirl of politics, motives, and desires, some might argue that the charter movement signals a perfect storm of low-income parents' desperate desire for educational justice mobilized and accelerated by anti-union, anti-government, and pro-choice interests.

For decades, the ideology of "choice" has variously attached to magnet schools, alternative schools, vouchers, and then charters. Historically, "choice" has been in conversation with concerns about equity, access, and accountability. Choice in its many forms has been seen by reformers across the political spectrum as a way of improving the performance of public education. While the most popular conservative policy banner for education choice has been vouchers, it is also true that the value of choice and participation has been at the heart of progressive educational reform. Small school and alternative school educators and advocates argued for "choice" within public school systems (Meier, 2005). Choice has also been the framework for building systems of racial integration, bringing together youth from across racially segregated district lines (Anand, Fine, Perkins, Surrey, & Kinoy, 2001; Orfield, 2001). Presently, however, the discourse of choice and public education has been appropriated almost entirely to focus on charter schooling and vouchers—even for students currently enrolled in religious schools or home-schooled.

Charters and testing as the favored mechanisms for public school innovation and improvement were legislatively encoded by the Obama administration. In the Race to the Top initiative sponsored by the federal government, states deemed eligible for funding cannot have any cap on the number of charters in the state and cannot have any law that would interfere with tying teacher promotion, tenure, or salary to test scores. By mobilizing such a powerful federal role in education, with substantial financing, this administration has become a major advocate for charters and for standardized testing. Secretary of Education Arne Duncan, joined by President Obama, insists on validating and financing the charter movement as an innovative stimulant to improve *public school systems*. Critically, a mist lingers over the questions we posed earlier regarding common understanding of "what's public." The question *Are charter schools public?* is complex. Although funded by tax-levy money—and then some—they often have selective admissions criteria, but so do a number of "successful" urban public schools; some parents, communities, boards, and hedge-fund entrepreneurs have a voice, but local communities and educators usually have little. Charter schools are, unevenly, accountable to state requirements. And so we begin with the presumption that charters are public, and yet, as you will read, significant questions remain unanswered about money, profit, access, pushouts, governance, accountability, and sustainability.

## WHAT IS AT STAKE?

At present only a very small segment of all schools are charter schools; they represent a tiny fraction of the children and the school buildings that constitute public education. And yet it is curious that with all the attention focused on charters as the policy engine for public education reform, few are asking about the consequences for neighborhood schools. In New York City, we witness a gross campaign for school closings and what is called co-location: moving charters into public school spaces where they "share" facilities and resources but most local children aren't eligible for admission. A zero-sum game of resource allocation means that charters expand and traditional schools (often their "neighbors") are declared as failed. The closure of schools and their reopening as charters, as well as the "co-location" of charters in public school buildings, have started to rip communities of color apart:

> March 2010: When hundreds of parents went to Albany last month to rally for charter schools, they were greeted by a parade of politicians offering encouragement and promises. But when Bill Perkins, the state senator from Harlem who represents many of the parents, took the stage, they drowned him out with boos . . . chanting, "Move, Bill, get out the way, get out the way," before he could even speak. As advocates of charter schools, including the Bloomberg administration, try to persuade legislators to lift the limit on the number of such schools in the state, no one is as likely to stand in their way as Mr. Perkins, whose district encompasses nearly 20 charter schools. Several more are planned next year. Over the last decade, as charter schools have multiplied, Mr. Perkins has undergone a dramatic shift and emerged as their most outspoken critic in the Legislature, writing guest columns in newspapers and delivering impassioned speeches criticizing the "privatization" of public schools. When officials of the city's Department of Education announced last year that they planned to place a charter school inside the Public School 123 building in Harlem, Mr. Perkins was infuriated. With help from his chief of staff, several parents and teachers' union representatives

staged a protest there on the first day of school, holding signs that labeled charter schools as "separate and unequal." Mr. Perkins recently announced plans to hold public hearings on charter schools, to examine, among other things, the sources of their financing and "how much profit there is in not-for-profit" schools. (Medina, 2010b, p. A22)

Not only do these strategic policy decisions pit neighbor against neighbor, but charters' record of selective student access and retention, with disproportionately low rates of English language learners, academically struggling and special education students, and with high discharge rates, is especially salient in determining if the public education goal of equity across race, class, and learning needs is being met.

## THE STRUCTURE OF THE BOOK

This book analyses the current conditions of public education through the lens of the charter movement, sorting out the promise of charter schooling from its recent record. Our intention is to take seriously the promises that have been made, the desperation of parents that has been tapped, the implications for the millions left behind, and the fundamental question of what is *public* in a nation at war, in decline, and in economic crisis? We need to understand how charters are also a political instrument, a wedge for radically transforming public schooling and all things public, as we have historically understood it.

Chapter 2, The Promise: The Genesis of Expectation and Challenge of Charter Reform, describes the *promise* of charter advocates regarding innovation, access, academic performance, and efficiency. Many of the assumptions regarding charters as an instrument for learning innovation and the multiplier benefits to public school systems are based on market dynamics of choice and competition. At the same time, charter schools' intent to create union-free environments "liberating" managers and teachers from inefficient and counterproductive regulations that erode academic performance has had much appeal. These market promises regarding choice are coupled with a belief that charters would function as engines for social justice.

From the point of view of parents in low-income communities, charters were sold and seen by many as a beacon of hope. Open access to all potential students, rigorous standards, responsiveness to community definition of educational need, and economic investment in the classroom and nieghborhood were all elements of the justice promise. Importantly, it was assumed that improved academic performance and access could be accomplished with no new economic investment but rather through a radical deregulation of public education. In sum, charters were seen as combining robust market alternatives to traditional public schools with social justice commitments to equalizing opportunity for the poorest students. Thus it is imperative to consider the evidence.

Chapter 3, The Tension Between the Promise and Evidence, discusses a range of studies that have been conducted both nationally and locally. The most prominent longitudinal national study was conducted by CREDO, a project of Stanford University. It sampled almost a million-and-a-half students in 15 states. Equally important, studies have been conducted in a cross-section of urban areas. Each of these research projects measured changes in the test scores of students in charters and public schools over varying amounts of time. In the aggregate, charters are not outperforming public schools on standardized-testing measures. There is much variation within the charter sector; selectivity in admissions and pushouts are significant equity concerns. Equally important, the promise of charters to ensure open access to a cross-section of students, allocate scarce resources away from management functions and into the classroom, and spur innovation that over time benefits public school systems is frequently refuted by available evidence. Clearly, exemplary charter schools have fulfilled many of these promises. The promise of charters, however, was not made for a few high-performing schools. A consideration of the evidence is especially important in an era when charters' numbers are rapidly expanding because of narratives of success embroidered on the fabric of the exceptional.

Chapter 4, Interlocking Power and the Deregulation of Public Education, considers the factors that account for the political success of the charter movement when the space between promise and evidence is so large. How, for example, have movement leaders managed to marshal ever-greater support for the expansion of charters? The chapter analyzes the interlocking economic, political, and social forces underpinning the charter movement. More to the point, the relationship between the packaging of education as a private good, the economic incentives of expanding charter schools, and the political support engendered by media and economic power are discussed. The often contradictory relationship between the economic and political logic of charter reformers and the requirements of building an effective reform agenda for public education are also considered. The attack on teacher unions must also be incorporated into any discussion of the growing power and success of charter school advocates.

Chapter 5, "Crisis": A Moment for Dispossession and Profit, explores the often invisible dispossessing consequences of neoliberal urban policy, in general, and the proliferation of charters, in particular, on students and their communities and asserts that disinvestment and dispossession reflect the underbelly of the innovation argument. We contrast Du Bois's analysis of our ongoing, relentless attack on, and "crisis" within, the Black community with Naomi Klein's analysis of shock doctrine and how "crisis" is manufactured as an opportunity for privatization. We explore the implications of "crisis" and charter rescue in Chicago, New Orleans, and New York City—analyzing both the ideological chants and the lives left behind, on the ground, searching for a good public school in neighborhoods now dotted with selective charters.

Chapter 6, Reclaiming "Public": Deepening National Commitments to Public Investment and Public Innovation, explores alternatives to present public education reform that pins most if not all of its hopes on charter schooling. This final chapter begins with a brief discussion of a public education as a public good and what differentiates it from market goods, what is lost and gained when we try to convert a public good into a market commodity. Equally important, the chapter explores systems of education in the United States and other parts of the world that have increased rates of literacy and numeracy, critical thinking, and social engagement. Finally, the development of such a system cannot occur without either targeted economic investment or progressive political power. Presently, however, both of these items are in short supply in the public discourse and political contestation regarding the future of public education. A brief final discussion will consider correctives to the present imbalance in power and policy remedy.

# CHAPTER 2

# The Promise:
# The Genesis of Expectation and
# the Challenge of Charter Reform

In the aftermath of the economic meltdown of 2008–2009, David Brooks (2009, October) a senior, politically conservative columnist for *The New York Times,* indicated, "The economy seems to be stabilized but people are anxious about America's future." Brooks suggested that if America is to maintain its competitive edge it must "revive innovation." The first priority for restoring the preeminent position of the American economy is to enact President Obama's education reforms. According to Brooks, we must "first push hard to fulfill reforms embraced by Republicans and Democrats, encourage charter-school innovation . . . that is the surest way to improve human capital." What Brooks captured in this single column is the confluence of economic and racial anxieties that have ignited charter school reform. He unites the failure of public school education with the declining economic status of America, suggesting that they both constitute a threat to America's historic way of life and that together they can lead us out of economic misery. This context of "profound unease" has provided a space of opportunity to inject radical market-driven reforms into the popular imagination and onto the landscape of public education. Charter schools are held ideologically as a vehicle for resurrecting, at once, public education and the economic dominance of American business.

The panic regarding public education has been in the air for decades. Yong Zhao, in *Catching up or Leading the Way* (2009), describes a simmering unrest with public education climaxing with the 1983 report *A Nation at Risk.* Quite pointedly, The National Commission on Excellence in Education indicated that America was at risk because of its poor education system. This damning portrait of American education has been enriched by international studies such as Trends in International Mathematics and Science Study (TIMSS) and the Program for International Student Assessment (PISA). Scholarly work and media reports describing the growing gap in test scores between U.S. students and other countries increasingly circulate. During the 20th anniversary of the report in 2003, it was announced that the education system remained as obsolete and broken as in 1983. Zhao suggests that the report defined education as a national security issue because of intensified economic competition for global dominance from Japan, China, and India. The federal response to the report has been woefully inadequate. Importantly, however, the report helped advance aggressive federal policies on matters of educational accountability and centralized standard setting; boosting business leaders' agenda of efficiency, market reform, and privatization. Perhaps most critically, the federal investment policy in public education might be characterized as the promulgation of a series of unfunded mandates. The most recent of these unfunded mandates during George W. Bush's presidency involved the implementation of No Child Left Behind (NCLB). This legislation's basic stated intention is to produce accountability through standardized testing in math and reading. It was the first initiative to truly bring the federal government as a regulator into American public education. Its substance and vision enjoy wide bipartisan and public support. As well, NCLB introduced principles of competition and choice into public education. The ever-louder drumbeat that poor test scores and failing schools largely accounted for the failing economy was a powerful impetus for both panic and reform. During these same years the federal and state prison expenditures skyrocketed, accounting for a dramatic realignment of federal and state investment from education to incarceration, a movement of Black and Brown bodies from schools to prisons, and a redistribution of opportunities and aspirations.

In a context of national and international educational anxiety, charter schools are being promoted as a kind of magic wand that will dramatically upgrade public school performance and, in turn, the economy. It is important to notice that charters are perceived as accomplishing these outcomes *at little if any additional cost* and at a time when federal and state contributions to school budgets are dropping precipitously. Race to the Top money represents a $4.35 billion increase in federal funding. If distributed equally across every state, it represents about an $80 million increase in revenue per state. Clearly, such investment is a drop in the bucket given the needs of public schools across the country. Alternatively, the decline in state and local public school allocations has been especially dramatic in the last year. A number of publications have projected substantial budget deficits for state governments and, in turn, a significant fiscal crunch for public schools. Symptomatic of the decline in funding is the job market for teachers, reported by the *New York Times* in May 2010: "The recession seems to have penetrated a profession long seen as recession proof. Teachers are facing the worst job market since the Great Depression. Amid state and local budget cuts cash poor urban districts like NYC and Los Angeles, which once hired thousands of young people every spring, have taken down the help wanted signs." The only exceptions to this trend: "Charter schools, which are publicly financed but independently run, are practically the only ones hiring in New York City and elsewhere because of growing enrollments and expanding political and economic support for school choice" (Hu, 2010, p. A1).

The potential of charters to transform public education, we are being told, is not through additional resources but through the freedom and flexibility to entertain and implement new, more effective approaches to education particularly in the poorest communities of color. Such expectation places an enormous weight on this single reform initiative. But it is precisely that expectation, in combination with the failures of and deep frustration with public education rightfully felt and expressed in poor communities of color that has produced a perfect storm for charter-school reform throughout the country.

Birthed at the precarious intersection of deep frustration in communities of color, high national anxiety, and ideological attacks on the public sphere, charters are the newest face of reform in the long U.S. history of public education. Charter reform has gained substantial momentum as a result of President Obama's legislative and oratorical support. With the introduction of the Race to the Top initiative, charter schooling is dominating much of the reform discourse regarding public education. This flood of government, media, and corporate support for this policy direction has occurred in a relatively short period. It is time to review the academic, social, and political impact of a movement that is well funded, has strong media support, is cascading through low-income communities, and now has the authority of the first Black president.

## THE LUSTER AND CONTRIBUTION OF
## EXEMPLAR CHARTER SCHOOLS

The charter school movement has stimulated a number of programs, generally perceived as exemplars. On the basis of documented evidence or innovative potential, these schools have been described as representing important pieces of the puzzle in the process of reassembling public education.

Perhaps the most widely recognized program nationally and internationally is Geoffrey Canada's Harlem Children Zone (HCZ). The program has imaginatively struggled to weave together anti-poverty programming, targeting a geographic area in Harlem with charter school instruction that works with children from pre-kindergarten through high school graduation. This comprehensive approach, which integrates family issues of health care, employment, and housing with academic development, is unique. Recently, the Obama administration indicated that it will borrow Canada's approach to launch Promise Neighborhoods as part of a comprehensive approach to ending poverty. The Harlem Children's Zone, however, as Canada admits, is a work in progress. He describes his agency's ambitious arc of aspiration by noting, "We won't have our cycle completed until ten years from now, it's a twenty year cycle." Importantly, "the Zone's Promise Academy schools have posted celebrated gain on the NYS standardized tests" (Zelon, 2010). More recently, the larger question of the HCZ's impact on poverty has, to date, eluded measurement. As was recently noted, the White House and the media have anointed the Harlem Children's Zone the model of choice for solving poverty, although it remains unclear what difference HCZ has made (Zelon, 2010).

On the other side of the continent in Los Angeles, Steve Barr and the Green Dot network of charter schools have made impressive differences in the academic performance of inner city youngsters of color. The entrepreneurial saga of leadership, challenge, and perseverance at the Animo Leadership Charter High School has been widely publicized. The leadership sacrifices are described as follows:

> Barr hired five of seven teachers straight out of college and rented classrooms at a night school. When one of the teachers quit in the first couple of weeks he replaced her with his office manager. Barr worked mostly without pay for the next few years spending the last of his savings . . . and doing such damage to his finances that COSTCO revoked his membership. (McGray, 2009, p. 69)

The climax to this story is not shot in the soft light of effort but rather the more radiant sunlight of academic improvement. In a relatively brief period, the Green Dot academy under Steve Barr's leadership was able to produce impressive results:

> At the end of the first chaotic year, Barr's school beat Hawthorne High School in every measurable outcome. "When the test scores come out, I have to call Shalvey"—Barr's charter-schools mentor—and ask him, "Are they good" Barr said. "Cause I don't fucking know. I don't know how to read test scores." Last year, *US News and World Report* ranked it among the top hundred high schools in the country. (McGray, 2009, p. 69)

Other national not-for-profit networks of charter schools such as KIPP (Knowledge is Power Program) and Uncommon Ground have attracted congratulatory media coverage. Uncommon Ground, which has a network of schools in New Jersey, New York City, and upstate New York, has also worked to develop a common curricula to ensure testing success. Their 300-page manual "details a wide range of techniques teachers should use in their classrooms, including six different types of questions they're expected to ask their students" (Toch, 2009b, p. 12).

Charter schools developed by the University of Chicago have labored to create curricula less defined by structures to promote testing outcomes than by an "effort to create an existence proof that ambitious intellectual work—and the kinds of instruction and social support it requires—can be implemented at scale" (Payne & Knowles, 2009). The program is incubating 20 schools with this curriculum, pre-K through 12th grade, across some of the most difficult districts in the South and West sides of Chicago. The objective is ultimately to serve ten thousand students per year. The architects of the program, Payne and Knowles (2009), recently noted:

> In the last year, the University of Chicago Charter Schools were named to the Illinois Honor Roll for being one of nine high-poverty, high performing schools in Chicago that are beating the achievement gap. Our newest elementary school, Donoghue was one of ten elementary charter schools nationwide to receive an EPIC (Effective Practice Incentive Community) award for bringing about outstanding student achievement gains—the only charter school in Illinois to receive this recognition. (p. 236)

We do not doubt that specific schools have improved the academic performance of poor youngsters of color. Importantly, how results were achieved remains less clear than the differences that have been documented. Are these schools playing on a level economic and political playing field with public schools? To what extent are these charter schools admitting fewer students with special learning needs? How are these schools' performance on testing affected by the attrition of problem learners and their migration back to public schools? How has a singular focus on testing reliance resulted in the improvement of test scores at the expense of other forms of learning such as critical thinking? What kinds of education and capacity are a best fit with 21st-century market demands? The latter questions extend beyond the boundaries of charter schooling to the fundamental reliance on testing as the single barometer of academic capacity. However, improving testing results is both a rationale for charter expansion and the basis for identifying exemplars. We will return to these questions throughout the book.

However effective these examples of charter experimentation may be, what remains indisputable is that they are not representative of the larger aggregated experience of charter schooling. A number of studies have indicated that the academic outcomes of charter schools are at best no different than traditional public schools. By definition an exemplar is an outlier, not a normative experience. This is an important point precisely because the outlier or exemplar charter program has been used as a basis for selling charter schools as a national policy for public education reform. The policy of charter reform is built on the soft, shifting sand of exemplar performance and not the firmer foundation of aggregated evidence of success. We do not dispute the potential or real contribution of charter schools as a stimulus for experimentation. Like any other effectively un-proven experiment, however, it should be implemented selectively and thoughtfully before it is translated into national policy. This has not been the case. To the contrary, the success of a few charter exemplars has been the pivot and referent point for the rapid expansion of the charter school movement. Exemplary programs by definition are not representative of the larger universe of charter schools. Indeed, exemplary public schools are rarely used to paint a positive spin on urban public education. They are routinely bracketed as "the exception." Yet in the charter sector, this is precisely what is occurring, as a number of political and economic interests advance an agenda of rapid expansion of charters to both replace and, presumably, inspire innovation within traditional public education.

## A HISTORY OF CHARTERS IN THREE MOVEMENTS

> The charter school idea was to create better schools for all children, not to divide limited public resources across parallel systems that perform at similar levels and suffer from similar breaches in accountability. . . . Once dedicated to educational quality, today's charter school move-ment is increasingly dominated by powerful advocates of market-based reform and privatization in public education. Quantity is the enemy of quality in the charter marketplace. (Miron & Dingerson, 2009, p. 30)

Early in the discourse of choice and public education, vouchers were per-ceived by many policy makers, particularly conservative advocates, as the preferred trigger for school reform. By providing cash value for each child's education, vouchers expected to promote transactions of choice and, in turn, best fit between student and school. Critical to this discus-sion, vouchers were an early forerunner of later choice initiatives such as charter schools. It was argued that by providing students a voucher value for their public education and, in turn, allowing consumers to make a market choice regarding their expenditure, the best schools would flourish while the worst disappeared. Over time, vouchers met stiff resistance from a cross-section of community groups, unions, and policy makers because of the attendant redistribution of public dollars to private schools—often church-related private schools—and the inequity of more affluent families building on the value of the voucher to provide an ever-more-elite education to their children, while poor families were once again relegated on the basis of their relatively meager voucher resources to the least desirable options.

It was within this context that progressive education reformers including Joe Nathan and union leaders like Albert Shanker agreed, in 1988, that charter schools could be an effective mechanism for incubating reform and improvement in a small number of experimental schools. In turn, it was expected that the charter experience in promoting innovation could be systematically disseminated to a much larger number of public schools. Below we present the history of the charter reform movement in three stages.

## Charters as Progressive, Experimental, Public Education Alternatives

At first, charter advocates sketched a set of ideas regarding institutional autonomy and flexibility they expected would result in experimentation and, in turn, improve academic performance, equitable access, and curricular innovation. The early movement focused on schools being chartered and publicly funded through legislative decree; assured the flexibility of autonomy necessary to experiment and improve academic performance. Nathan is often credited with launching the first modern-day charter options in Minnesota in 1991. He articulated social justice principles for both structuring and assessing the performance of charters:

1.  Charters are public, nonsectarian, free, and open to all without any admission tests or criteria.
2.  The charters will follow all civil laws and analogous democratic restraint.
3.  The charter frees up the school from rules about curriculum management and teaching in return for transparent accountability for results.
4.  The school is a discrete entity with its own board and site management.
5.  Employees have the right to organize and bargain collectively.
6.  The full per-pupil allocation of funds follows students to charters.

7. Teachers who join a charter are given the flexibility to return to the regular system and participate in programs such as state teacher-retirement systems. (Dingerson, Miner, Peterson, & Walters, 2008)

The early charters were often borne of commitments to social justice, trying to provide to marginalized youth what more privileged youth were getting in private schools—small schools, small classes, community ownership, dedicated faculty, and a multicultural and social justice curriculum. The bargain struck was an exchange of autonomy for accountability, measured presumably in terms of a rise in student test scores. Indeed many of the early charters reflected the progressive wisdom borne of the small-schools movement of the early 1980s (Cook & Tashlik, 2005; Meier, 2005). Albert Shanker threw his considerable political weight behind charter reform when he declared that they were an important incubator for needed education reform. Over time, however, he became increasingly skeptical about the potential of charters, noting they were, at best, a partial answer to the problems that afflict our schools and that, at worst, the basic premise of charter schools would ensure that whatever common ground schools then shared would disappear (Bracey, 2004).

This early promise of charters was tethered to the belief that by freeing a sector of schools from the red tape and formulaic practices of bureaucratized education, new forms of practice would be unleashed that, in turn, would improve academic performance. Such freedom was associated with the anticipated innovation and experimentation necessary to dramatically improve learning culture and outcomes of public education.

## The Philanthropic/Hedge-Fund Movement

This formulation of a small number of charters functioning as experimental, relatively autonomous programs was swept up in the 1990s by a movement organized to promote an ambitious alternative to public schools. More to the point, charter movement ideology veered to the Right. It increasingly emphasized charter schooling as an alternative to public education, identified teachers and their unions as primary culprits in the "decline" of academic achievement, and characterized the problem of public education as primarily a consequence of dysfunctional organizations while rendering invisible the inequitable distribution of resources to the poorest public school systems. These messages were filtered through a growing infrastructure of institutions allied to advance policies of charter schooling.

The first of these institutions to provide policy support for increased funding consisted of a cross-section of "think tanks." They were soon joined by state advocacy groups, foundations and networks of charter schools, or charter-management organizations (CMOs). Critically, the foundations included but were not limited to Gates, Walton, Broad, and Ohlin, which also provided supplementary funding to charters. It was within this context that a groundswell of media attention critiqued the record of public education and argued that only an abundance of autonomous alternatives could unleash the potential of schooling and students. In this moment the ever-louder voices of an increased number of movement "entrepreneurs" elevated charters as *the* policy alternative to the continuing wasteful investment of resources in public schools, asserting that as a nation we were throwing good money after bad in the education system. The authority of individual entrepreneurs committed to charter reform was bolstered by the resources and influence of a number of key foundations. The initial progressive direction and assumptions of charter pioneers were being steered by an ever-more-conservative ideological movement emphasizing the value of high-stakes testing, low-cost–short-term/transitory educators (with such programs as Teach for America), and the rapid proliferation of charters as a substitute for or alternative to public education.

By 2008, we began to see a widening web of influence by a growing network of charter advocates. Corporate educational "entrepreneurs," collaborating with conservative groups like Democrats for Education Reform, mounted organizing campaigns intended to discredit public schools and market charters in poor communities. Charters moved from an alternative within public education to an alternative pitched against public education.

An especially vivid example of such a campaign occurred in Harlem. With a small brochure published by Democrats for Education Reform in 2008, an unprecedented 3-month school choice campaign was launched in Harlem (Democrats for Education Reform, 2008). Democrats for Education Reform explained that "two obstacles have stood in the way of this important shift in the schooling marketplace: (1) a lack of clear understanding among parents that an increasing number of quality school options exists and (2) longstanding political allegiance to a failing public education status quo" (2008). They continue, "The idea was to flood the zone in Harlem with a school choice message in the period leading up to the neighborhood's charter school lotteries" (2008, pp. 2–3).

The campaign's results: More than 5,000 people showed up for the Success Charter Network lottery, where some 3,000 students applied for some 600 seats.

## Steroids from Obama

We find ourselves, in 2010, at the third stage of the charter movement. Charters have gained legitimacy, popular support, momentum, extensive media coverage, and, now, federal government sponsorship. As noted earlier, the movement received an enormous boost with the infusion of Race to the Top monies, which require states to lift their caps on charters. A number of states have complied with this federal directive and passed legislation enabling charter caps to be lifted. At the same time, the outcry against this strategy has been substantial and noticeable from some former charter advocates including, most prominently, Diane Ravitch, former assistant secretary of education (1991–1992).

## THE POLICY LANDSCAPE: COMMITMENTS AND VARIATION

To date, more than 5,000 charter schools are operating across 40 states and the District of Columbia, educating more than 1.5 million students. While this is indeed a sector and a movement, the laws and funding arrangements vary dramatically by state. As Leigh Dingerson (2008) demonstrates in her taxonomy, shown below, the charter landscape is wide and varied.

## THE CHARTER LANDSCAPE

### Free Market Charters

- Public education is seen as a "market opportunity" for entrepreneurs and business.
- Charters are seen as a vehicle to transfer public dollars to private hands.
- "Choice" defines parents as consumers and encourages individualistic behavior.
- Many of these operators are for-profit corporations and aim for quantity—sometimes operating dozens of schools.
- Chartering is used as a strategy to weaken teacher unions and as a political wedge issue in low-income communities of color.

*Examples:* White Hat Managements, K–12, Edison Schools, Inc.

### "Mom and Pop" Charters

- Schools are run by experienced educators, frustrated with the district bureaucracy and trying to model a different kind of educational strategy for disadvantaged kids.
- The schools are usually small.
- They tend to be single schools and may have deep community roots.
- They may have a special focus—cultural or pedagogic focus— or they may fill a particular niche that is underserved in the public district.

*Examples:* Dolores Huerta, Denver; Next Step PSC, Washington; Folk Arts/Cultural Treasures, Philadelphia. These schools in general are focused on elementary-age children.

### Franchises

- These are usually large nonprofit operations that attempt to bring charters "to scale."
- They differ a little from the free market types because they typically have an educational theory (for better or worse) as compared to, *primarily*, a market rationale/ideology.
- Schools often have a unique model or culture and are replicated in cookie-cutter style across a district or nationally. (Center for Community Change, 2008)

*Examples:* Green Dot, most are in California; Knowledge Is Power Program (KIPP), charter networks serving children from kindergarten through high school.

Across types of charters, the basic contract between the state and charter schools involves an agreement between the school's founding group and government authorizer(s). This contractual agreement of authorization is critical to the development of standards, types, and quantity of schools. Those states with the most decentralized decision making also have the fewest centralized regulations for enforcing basic standards. Ohio, for instance, has more authorizing agencies than any state in the country. Linda Darling-Hammond notes that approximately 65 authorizing agencies exist in the state, and about 50% of the charter schools in Ohio are sponsored by nonprofit entities unconnected with any public agency (2009). A consequent explosion in the number of charters in Ohio has led to very serious concerns about quality and accountability.

We review here a series of policy dimensions promulgated and enforced by state and local governments. These lenses are essential to understanding the differential evolution of charters across the country. As well, they represent the crucial fault lines of key public questions, including, Are charters public? To whom are charters accountable? Whose school is this anyway?

## POLICY DIMENSIONS:
## ARE CHARTER SCHOOLS PUBLIC INSTITUTIONS?

### Who Authorizes Charters?

The reach and status of local authorizing agencies or legally granting charter status varies substantially. For example, state law determines what bodies have the authority to authorize a charter school. These bodies range from school districts to state departments of education to public universities to private nonprofits. The role of the authorizer is to solicit proposals for charters, review the proposals, grant or deny the charters, and oversee/monitor schools' compliance with their charter agreements and state law. With but one exception in state law, only nonprofits can apply for a charter. The charter school must be run by a governing board. However, and this is an increasingly important point, the governing board of the nonprofit charter-holder can then subcontract the management of the school to a for-profit Education Management Organization (EMO) or nonprofit Charter Management Organization (CMO). Such contracts can also place any part of the school's management, from simply handling payroll to running the whole school, under the CMO/EMO control.

In Maryland, only local school districts can authorize charters. Wisconsin, California, Michigan, and Arizona permit for-profit corporations to manage charters. Minnesota permits a wide range of authorizing agencies including school boards, public and private colleges, and district cooperatives but, unlike many other states, requires that teachers have a majority of seats on the charter school board.

Other states including New York and New Jersey have developed more centralized mechanisms for granting charters. One expression of such centralized oversight has been placing strict limitations on the number of charters that can be authorized. For example, in New York state, the ceiling as of January 2010 was 200, but it was raised to 400 during the 2010 legislative session in response to federal insistence that eligibility for Race to the Top and Innovation Fund monies requires that charter restrictions be eased.

## How Autonomous Are Charters?

Alex Molnar notes that one of the most important differences between charter-school laws is the degree of autonomy granted to the schools. A number of states have been guided by the notion that for charters to be successful in promoting both innovation and improved student outcomes, they must have a maximum degree of deregulation from public bureaucracies, or autonomy. For example, the Center for Education Reform national charter "think tank" emphasizes maximal deregulation and advocates (a) setting charters aside in the creation and oversight from the conventional system, (b) permitting independent, distinct entities to open schools and hold them accountable, and (c) not requiring adherence to the layers of oversight of conventional public schools (see Center for Education Reform website, http://www.edreform.com/Home/). It is on this basis that the Center for Education Reform described Arizona, Colorado, Massachusetts, Michigan, and Colorado as having strong charter laws, "because they allow these schools to operate as independent legal entities with a high degree of autonomy" (Center for Education Reform website). Alternatively, states concerned with the implications associated with creating an alternative system of charter schools that are autonomous with respect to public agencies have more restrictive legislation. It is within this context that charter school laws passed in Hawaii, Georgia, Kansas, New Mexico, and Wyoming are described as weak, because "they grant charters little more autonomy than public schools" (Molnar, 1996, p. 52).

Parenthetically, many public schools, especially those in the small schools movement, have been advocating for flexibility and autonomy in exchange for rich, complex forms of transparency and accountability and have been rebuffed for decades (see Cook & Tashlik, 2005; Fine, 1991; Meier, 2005).

## What Is the Length of a Charter Contract?

A critical issue for authorization is the length of time that a contract runs. Reauthorization is a means of focusing on the performance of charters over a specific period of time. Generally speaking, the longer the contract, the more lax is the enforcement of standards regarding school performance. Minnesota law limits a charter contract to 3 years. California requires renewal every 5 years. Alternatively, charters in Arizona and Washington, DC, are granted for 15 years. Most charters are contracted for 3 to 5 years before being renewed.

## Are There Statewide Caps on Charter Development?

The question of caps on charter development is politically contentious, particularly in the aftermath of new incentives developed through Race to the Top to lift caps. To date, according to the National Alliance for Public Charter Schools, 26 states and Washington, DC, have established a cap on the number of charter schools. Gary Miron and Leigh Dingerson (2009) published an important editorial in *Education Week*: "Time to get off the expansion express: Is proliferation of the charter-school market interfering with its quality?" They argue that the rapid proliferation of charter schools appears to be inversely related to charter performance. Drawing on the Stanford University Center for Research on Education Outcomes (CREDO) study (described in detail below), the authors conclude that "state level findings from this study suggest that quantity [of charters] is the enemy of quality in the charter marketplace" (Center for Research on Education Outcomes, 2009). A close state-by-state examination of the CREDO report suggests that "states with the most charter schools are also most likely to be found in the poor performing group while states with few charters tended to cluster among the most successful. Specifically, states with positive student achievement growth had only 61.6 charters on average, while states with negative growth had an average of 275 charter schools" (2009). As it turns out, "in the poorly performing states a much higher proportion of charter schools are run by for-profit EMOs" (2009).

## To Whom Are Charters Accountable?

Effective monitoring is critical to holding charters accountable to their promise of increasing academic achievement, maximizing responsible fiscal management of resources, offering equity of access, and promoting dissemination of their innovations to public schools. Such oversight and enforcement of standards has, however, been very difficult to accomplish. For example, multisite networks of charters tend to create reporting structures that obscure fiscal and disaggregated student performance data. In part, this is a consequence of intensified competition between networks for scarce public resources and incentives to conceal discovery and data from competitor networks. As well, some part of this flawed reporting may be a consequence of networks not having developed effective data management. In a number of states such as Arizona, California, and Ohio it has been difficult to gain access to fiscal data.

Jeffrey Henig, a professor at Columbia University, notes the irony:

> The state and local leaders who are pushing most aggressively for . . . charters and choice have not made it a priority to link their initiatives to requirements for public dissemination of data and staged implementation. In an environment of low information and exaggerated claims, the risks of doing damage are as important to consider as the problematic advantages of precipitous and undigested reform. (Bracey, 2005, p. 6)

Nonetheless, by 2009, 12.5% of the more than 5,000 charter schools established in the United States had closed because of financial, management, and academic reasons or what is called district interference (Center for Education Reform, 2009).

## CHARTERS, THE MARKETPLACE, AND A THEORY OF CHANGE

We have tracked the history of charters through the education reform lineage, but there is, of course, another lineage through which the charter movement has gained steam: the privatization and transformation of the public sphere accompanied by the massive encroachment of for-profit management into public affairs. Historically, competition has been described by economists as the primary force for change within market environments. Markets, economies, and capitalism, as Hayek and Harvey suggest, are engaged in an ongoing process of creative destruction that is stimulated and fed by competition. The logic suggests that those businesses, unable to compete on the basis of the quality of their product, pricing or profits, will ultimately be destroyed, as more efficient and innovative corporations emerge on the basis of heightened productivity and/or more effective products. It is on this basis that corporations prevail or are vanquished in the marketplace. Competitive edge is often a consequence of greater use of labor-saving technology (computers); re-engineered products like Blu-ray films and creating better fit with the tastes and needs of consumers; expansion of research and development (R & D) investments structured to yield new products, such as iPods; and opening new markets. It is within such a context that market competition has been portrayed as unleashing the creative or innovative forces that ultimately benefit consumers. The trigger of competition is seen by many as a synonym for efficiency, innovation, and effectiveness.

The stimulant of market choice and competition as the singular force for redrawing the boundaries and prospect of public education raises a number of important questions.

- How does the introduction of business models of competition into school systems effectively redefine the collaborative function and purposes of a public system of education?
- As competition intensifies between schools for increasingly scarce resources, how will the process of distributing resources be politicized?
- Equally important, if testing is the sole criterion for resource allocation, what impact does that have on the quality and content of curriculum and pedagogy in public education?
- When a school is losing its students because of competitive disadvantages, is there any certainty that it will respond by improving its practices or performance? Or is it just as likely that reduced funding and greater concentration of the poorest-performing students will lead to a downward spiral in performance and, in turn, school closings?
- What impact does this have on peer effects, or the migration of the best students out of traditional public schools and the consequence of the lowest performing students internalizing reduced standards?
- Finally, how does an ethic of competition accord with the collective purposes of a public system of education?

## THE APPEAL OF CHARTERS TO DOMINANT ECONOMIC INTERESTS: MONETIZING PUBLIC EDUCATION

The language of "market share," like the logic of choice, competition, and transformative change, is resonant with both the ideology and experience of the corporate sector and for-profit public education. Eva Moscowitz, a "charter school entrepreneur," captures both the language and aspiration of transforming public education into a marketplace commodity:

> We plan to open our last three [charter schools] in Harlem in August 2010 and then move to Bronx. . . . With 27 charters in Harlem [counting other non–Harlem Success charter schools] we will have market share and will have fundamentally changed the rules of the game. (cited in Gonzalez, February 25, 2010)

Consistent with the intent to marketize public education, in 2009 the *New York Times* reported that hedge-fund managers are upping their investment of time and money in charter schools of their choosing. Moskowitz, a manager of a network of charters in Harlem and a former NYC councilwoman, noted, "These guys get it, they aren't afraid of competition or upsetting the system, they thrive on it" (Hass, 2009). The market ethos of investment and return is translated by two hedge-fund managers to public schools:

> The schools are exactly the kind of investment people in our industry spend our days trying to stumble on. . . . With incredible cash flow even if in this case we don't ourselves get any of it. It's the most important cause in the nation, obviously, and with the state providing so much of the money outside contributions are insanely well leveraged. (Hass, 2009)

The confluence of market dynamics, such as public-school choice (in various iterations) and competition with business leader support, has created a space for monetizing public education. This should come as no surprise. What better way to intensify competition, promote efficiencies, and presumably heighten productivity than to insert businesspeople into public-education transaction, not simply as policy makers or fund-raisers, but as purveyors of goods and services?

Critically, the motivations of social entrepreneurs in this field are complex. Many are involved in advancing social purposes, for example, the academic development of the poorest youngsters in urban areas. Others see charters as a political and/or ideological opportunity to open up the public sector to market forces. Still others see it as an opportunity to accumulate capital or wealth and/or break the backs of the teachers' unions. Importantly, many of the social entrepreneurs engaged in this work have internalized a number of these beliefs and act upon them simultaneously. That said, part of the promise of charters is opening public education as a new market for private entrepreneurs. Pauline Lipman suggests that even nonprofit, managed charters in Chicago serve as centers of profit making:

> Limited resources have forced many charters to contract out school administration to EMO's (nonprofit) who create funding partnerships with business people or corporations. (Lipman, 2002)

Like charter law, charter financing arrangements vary from state to state. In most states, charters are allocated a percentage of the per-capita/per-child funding. But charter schools are often in receipt of substantial external support from private donors or philanthropy. A national analysis of charter school finance, conducted by the Thomas B. Fordham Institute, a charter-advocacy group, reports that charter schools in 16 states and Washington, DC, on average receive 20% less per child than traditional public schools receive. The study finds that the funding gap growing in urban districts, with charters lacking access to capital funding.

The lower per capita reimbursement received by charters is at least partially subsidized by foundations and patrons. Tom Toch, in his report on the movement to scale up the "Nations Best Charter Schools," notes, "CMO business plans reveal that nearly every prominent charter network is heavily reliant on philanthropy to cover costs" (2009a, p. 28). This point is further illustrated by the following anecdote:

> To fill the gap leading CMO's have turned to philanthropy. It has taken over a half a billion in philanthropy to sustain the CMO movement over the past decade. Some funds have come from high profile events—in 2006 the NYC Robin Hood foundation raised nearly 48 million dollars in a single night— from Wall Street moguls, Jay Z and Beyonce, and celebrities like Tom Brokaw and Jon Stewart. But the bulk of the philanthropic funding comes from five foundations, Broad, Dell, Fisher, Gates, and Walton. . . . Gates alone has given charter management organizations at least 136 million . . . a couple of years ago. (Toch, 2009a, p. 14)

An increasing number of foundations such as Gates, Walton, and the Broad family philanthropies have poured more than $600 million into charter schooling. As well, private patrons not necessarily affiliated with foundations, often from Wall Street and hedge-fund management, have also invested in charter schooling. This private money both adds to the revenue base of publicly funded programming and, in other instances, is the sole source of income for functions such as infrastructure. These practices and trends, however, raise a number of vexing questions, for example:

- How does this penetration of and dependence on private money influence the practices of schools?
- What kinds of tensions are created between charter accountability to larger, often more anonymous public structures that continue to provide the largest part of their revenue and private donors?
- If the lever of private financing is available to supplement funding, does it offer advantages to specific "anointed" charter schools and disadvantage traditional schools as well as the largest number

of charters? (For example, the Harlem Children Zone's per-capita investment in each of its students is three times the level of per-capita investment for the New York City school system.)

- Often charters touted as exemplary are receiving a combination of public and private allocations that exceed per-capita public allocations. Shouldn't that be part of the lesson of charter schooling?
- If exemplary charter schools require greater financing, then don't all public schools and charters merit similar investment?

These questions rarely if ever enter the present policy debate.

The greater reach of private foundations and patrons into public schools is likely to be an expansive trend in the near future. Clearly, in periods of economic crisis the reach of a small group of patrons having access to substantial resources and intently focused on reshaping public-education policy is likely to penetrate the independent decision-making authority of the state. In turn, such a dynamic further blurs the boundaries separating dominant economic groups such as affluent patrons, foundations, and corporations and government. In 2010 a number of foundations contributed to the public school contract settlement in Washington, DC. As the *Washington Post* recently reported, the preliminary agreement includes a voluntary individual performance-pay program financed largely by private foundations. A similar grant was provided by Facebook founder Mark Zuckerberg in Newark.

Clearly, this giving is structured to achieve objectives that overlap with those of the charter movement. To begin with, the role of teacher unions is undermined because patron commitment to individual forms of merit-pay compensation based on testing outcomes is in direct tension with the historically more collective forms of bargaining agreement negotiated with the state. This tension is especially taut in periods of resource scarcity. Secondly, this funding is ultimately not accountable to local forms of control. Democratic accountability to a city council or a neighborhood citizen-group is less clear because the money stands outside the public domain as does the larger policy directive about how the money must be spent. The nexus of economic power and public education policy is especially troubling because of the democratic role that schools have played in the life of American communities. The concentration of influence comes with significant costs to any aspiration for a more open and democratic public space.

## THE QUESTION OF MONEY AND CORRUPTION

As public education is monetized in the marketplace it is increasingly vulnerable to new forms of corruption. The following anecdote vividly illustrates this point:

> Maybe they should have just paid with a credit card. Three city charter schools are on the hook for thousands of dollars in interest payments to a for-profit management company. Victory Schools Inc. charges charter schools between $2,000 and $2,700 a student for back office support and help with curriculum planning and hiring. But if the schools can't pay up, they get socked. The company charged more than $100,000 in interest payments to three of its schools last year alone, using rates ranging from 6% to about 15% if a school pays late. (Kolodner, 2010)

Large private investments in public institutions have historically leveraged special privileges. In this instance, because of the size of their giving, a few foundations and patrons have the potential to influence both the development of specific charter networks and the reform direction of public school policy. It is within this context that some have referred to Bill Gates as the shadow secretary of education. It may be important to recall that the Bill and Melinda Gates Foundation was a key philanthropic supporter of the early small schools movement, working closely with coalitions of progressive small schools across the nation. At some point in the romance with small schools, however, program officers at Gates grew impatient and pressed for a rapid rise in test scores and an accelerated scaling up process. Both of these goals ran contrary to the small schools' ethical and professional commitments to performance assessment, and schools designed and cultivated over time by dedicated committees of educators and community members. The romance ended abruptly. Soon thereafter, Gates turned their support to the charter schools movement. This dynamic of philanthropy-driven initiatives and a changing of foundation priorities raises a number of questions about accountability. To begin with, to whom are charters accountable—a public governing body or private patrons? How do we collectively balance the democratic purposes of public education and the dominance of a few patrons and foundations over policy-making? To what extent has the growing voice of dominant economic and political interests facilitated the silencing of diverse voices, particularly poor people of color? Finally, isn't the direction and magnitude of such giving creating a "Tale of Two School Systems"—one with access to private resources and the other increasingly starved? Journalist and NPR commentator Juan Gonzalez notes:

> The design of charters will marshal resources by any means possible; they are designed structurally to guarantee the flourish of corruption, we are going to see more. Charter policy is simply structured to guarantee corruption. (Gonzalez, 2010)

## SCALING UP REFORM THROUGH A NETWORK OF CHARTERS: THE TRADEOFFS OF EFFICIENCY—AND ECONOMIC ADVANTAGE

Increasingly, charter authorization and accountability are conducted through networks of charters organized through education- or charter-management organizations (EMOs/CMOs). The number of EMOs has rapidly increased during the past decade. As noted earlier, today there are an estimated five thousand charter schools enrolling a million and a half students nationally (Miron & Dingerson, 2009). That number increased over a 5-year period by approximately 60% (Miron & Dingerson, 2009). In 1998 and 1999, a total of 61 charter schools were managed by nonprofit CMOs nationally. By 2008 and 2009, that number had swelled to 609. Equally important, in 2008 and 2009, 733 charter schools were managed by for-profit EMOs. That number doubled over an approximate 5-year period (Molnar, Garcia, Miron, & Berry, 2007). Sixty-one EMOs are organized as both for-profit and nonprofit entities. The scaling up of charter reform from individual schools to network is widely assumed to be the only way to ensure the economies of scale necessary to fulfill the infrastructural needs of charters including but not limited to billing departments, technology support services, record keeping, and teacher training that might otherwise be unavailable. As we add these functions to charter schooling through the increased scale of networks ranging from five to hundreds of schools, the entire movement is faced with a dilemma. On the one hand, the charter movement promised that its decentralized, individual, "experimental" schools would deliver more effective instruction because autonomy from public bureaucracy would promote flexibility and innovation. On the other hand, as charters transition from individual unaffiliated schools or small networks to ever-larger networks, they face the prospect of reproducing new forms of bureaucracy and, thus, the very same impediments to innovation its proponents argue in large part explains the failures of public education. In sum, the very "flexibility" and "innovation" credited to charters are more likely to be undermined in large networks, managed from afar, with strict codes of enforcement and steep back office fees.

Michael Mulgrew, president of the New York United Federation of Teachers, described a conversation with New York State charter advocates vividly illustrating the tension between profit and quality in public education:

> I am having to learn about a new concept—per pupil back office management fees. This is what the for profit charter management groups are charging schools to manage their schools. There was a school in Brooklyn where the management fee was $1,800 a kid, and then a school in Buffalo where they were charging $5,000 per kid. These guys are just using the schools to make money. So I offered for the UFT to partner with the Charter advocates; said we could go to Albany together and we could lobby for equal funding for children in charters, but I would only do that if they agreed to remove for profit managers from their Boards. They said no deal. The equal funding isn't worth it. So you got to be suspect about whose interests they are representing. (Mulgrew, 2010)

The rapid expansion of CMOs and EMOs as a management umbrella has been part of a systematic effort by think tanks, foundations, and some state governments to expand charter schooling. Ironically, as Bracey suggests, schools run by EMOs often "offer no curricular freedom or building level decision making whatsoever" (2004). The evolution of charters into regional and national networks does, however, signal recognition among leaders of the opportunities associated with scale and geographic reach. The question is—opportunities for what?

The demand for expansion has produced a number of dilemmas. For example, Miron and Dingerson indicate that there is an inverse relationship between the rapid proliferation of charters and rates of student achievement (2009). They also indicate that in the poorly performing states, a much higher proportion of charters is run by for-profit EMOs (2009).

## PARENTS' SEARCH FOR ALTERNATIVES TO A SYSTEM THAT HAS DISINVESTED

The language of choice has a powerful pull and meaning for parents who have witnessed the continuing disinvestment in, and therefore failure of local public schools to educate their children. Mapping onto a long history of African American parents seeking exit from the public sector, designing and flocking to alternatives to local schools, the history of exclusion, Jim Crow segregation, abuse, miseducation, and then Freedom Schools is too resonant. Allegiance to all-Black segregated schools-of-choice or to local parochial schools is well documented (Walker, 1996) Du Bois, Zora Neale Hurston, and Carter Goodwin have written extensively and with suspicion about the goals of traditional education for Black children.

Thus the appeal of an alternative to the existent public-school system is not lost on Black parents. As Juan Gonzalez, reporter for the *Daily News* suggested, charter schools are the new second tier, especially for African-American parents. More to the point, he asserts that charters are the new parochial schools, attractive to the upwardly mobile, low-income parent searching for an alternative (Gonzalez, 2010).

The first tier of schooling is reserved for the more affluent, White students in elite public or private schools. The second tier, or charters, offers a relatively scarce commodity reserved for a small number of poor students of color. Entrée is generally restricted to the relatively able student or knowledgeable parent. As part of a second tier, charters promise safer, elite-supported forms of education that will lead to more-successful career trajectories.

Importantly, the third tier is reserved for the majority of poor or working-class people of color, with frequent lack of access to decision makers, unresponsiveness of staff to breakdowns in learning and instruction, too frequent signs of disrespect to parents interested in rectifying their child's problems, and evidence that students are simply not mastering the skills necessary to compete in college or the marketplace. This experience has caused many families to search for an option to their local public schools. The most informed and resource-advantaged parents in poor neighborhoods may choose anyone of a number of exit options from urban public education, including but not limited to parochial schools and shuttling their child to a suburban district. Clearly, these parents are making decisions to advantage the educational and life-chance prospects for their individual children every day, by migrating their children out of failing public schools. Simultaneously, the overwhelming majority of poor students of color are, however, relegated to underfunded and overwhelmed inner-city public schools representing the lowest tier of education. For those left behind, the frustrations and ineffectiveness of neighborhood schools produces a festering resentment that grows and hardens.

The exit option is seen as a sign of hope and relief from the intergenerational dead-end experience of public schooling. It is within a context of failing public schools that a parent leader in Detroit, Sharlonda Buckman, recently suggested, "Somebody needs to go to jail . . . somebody needs to pay for this . . . and it shouldn't be the kids" (Esparza, 2009). Buckman is specifically suggesting that civil lawsuits and jailing should be enacted for anyone in the city's educational system who is not doing his or her job to properly educate children. In California, the Parent Union—supported by Broad Foundation funding and Green Dot charter organizing—has helped to craft and pass legislation referred to as the "parent trigger bill." The group claims that the bill forces school districts to completely overhaul a public school or turn it over to a charter if 51% of the parents vote for such change (Jessica Smith, personal communication, April, 2010). These are indeed desperate times, with "solutions" fed by a well-funded campaign to starve public education and feed the dismantling.

The promise of charters for many parents is therefore interlocked with a restoration of hope that their children can do better than the last generation; this promise reflects the hope that drives and explains their daily sacrifices. The effort of individual parents to secure a quality education for their children through charter schooling is both rational and escalating, but as a collective strategy it is a delusion. It is not surprising, as Pauline Lipman notes, that new educational options or a charter resonates with a swelling number of educators and families (Lipman, 2011, p. 389). The "good sense" in these policies is that they mandate decisive action to "turn around" a system that has profoundly failed to educate all students especially students of color (Lipman, 2011). This "sense making" is derived both from the parents' experiences and the language of advocates. More specifically, the agenda for charters and vouchers is often infused with a language of equity and justice. Equally important, school reform is often framed as a binary choice between justice, equity, innovation or accountability, and the failed policies of the past (Lipman, 2011). This powerful interlock between the frustration of parents and the language of hope and accountability offered by charter leaders has created a cascading demand to exit public schools and opt for charters.

The nexus between parent frustration and support for charter initiatives, however, is not simply a consequence of historic serendipity or the pure intentions of the charter movement. To the contrary, professionals, advocates, business interests, and a number of foundations have joined forces to channel this frustration into organized grassroots opposition to public education and support for charter schooling. This support is often contested by parent groups committed to preserving local control and neighborhood schooling. A recent especially powerful example of this splintering occurred in New Orleans. Charter parents were whipped into a frenzy because of a proposal to restore local control and the parish system. In October 2010 a public hearing was convened by the state board of education. The meeting according to those who attended turned into a screaming match between charter-school advocates and traditional, local school parents and advocates.

Clearly, meetings are being organized by the charter movement throughout the country, from Harlem to Los Angeles. Blame is tossed at teachers and schools for the failures of their children, while other groups of parents are fighting to halt school closings, stop for-profit companies like the Edison Project from assuming managerial control of buildings, and organizing campaigns to promote new and increased forms of investment in local public education. This parental push-pull is at the heart of the contested terrain of public schooling. If many parents are voting for charters with their feet as they leave public schools, as the false promise of charters comes to light, many others are fighting across the country for an enlarged investment and role in their local public schools (Fabricant, 2010, 2011a).

In the last year, the promise of charters as a solution to the crisis of public education has gained substantial momentum. No matter the promise, policy making over time must be informed by the record of charters on student achievement and the dissemination of their innovation to public schools. We will now turn our attention to a number of the empirical outcomes associated with charter education and the paradoxical policy response of silence regarding these important findings.

# CHAPTER 3

# The Tension Between Promise and Evidence

The policy promise of charters to improve test scores, enhance equity, and promote innovation is the focus of this chapter. How effective has the charter movement been in keeping these policy promises? Table 3.1 sketches the contours of the promise, the state of the evidence, and the academic citations for readers who seek to know more.

## THE PROMISE-EVIDENCE GAP

Here we review the straightforward empirical evidence on the impact of charter schools in terms of academic outcomes, equity, graduation/dropout rates, impact on neighboring public schools, college-going, teacher experience and turnover, and parental satisfaction. Responding to the elements of the promise articulated in Chapter 2, this chapter tries to pair, as systematically as possible, the available empirical evidence gathered from charter studies across the nation.

### Student Achievement: Test Score Achievement Data

Over the past few years, a number of national and city-specific studies demonstrate that on the basis of standardized testing results, charter performance is, in the aggregate, no better than that of public schools and often is worse.

In August 2004, *The New York Times* reported that data collected by the federal Department of Education "dealt a blow to supporters of the charter school movement" (Schemo, 2004). Fourth graders attending charter schools were lagging a half year behind their counterparts in public schools in both reading and math (2004). The results were based on the 2003 National Assessment of Educational Progress (NAEP), commonly known as the nation's report card. Chester Finn, a well-known advocate for charter

TABLE 3.1. The Promise and the Evidence

| Promise | Evidence | Citations |
|---|---|---|
| **STUDENT ACHIEVEMENT** | | |
| To what extent do charters improve student achievement in terms of<br>* Reading<br>* Math<br>* Graduation<br>* Dropout/ Push out<br>* College-going | The best evidence comes from the CREDO study: Most charters do as well as or less well than traditional public schools on achievement tests; 17% outperform local schools.<br><br>There are studies reviewing the same database that yield conflicting results (Hoxby, Muraka, & Kang, 2009; Reardon, 2009) There is some evidence of the positive impact of NYC charters but underenrollment of ELL and special education students makes comparisons to local schools difficult.<br><br>There are very few studies of charter attrition rates, dropout or push out, and graduation rates or college going, although there is substantial anecdotal information about high turn-over/push out rates, shifting class size across grade levels, and concerns voiced by parents that youth are being sent "back" to public schools mid-year. | Baker (2010); Barr, Sadovnik, & Visconti (2006); Bennett (2010), Bettinger (2005); Booker , Sass, Gill, & Zimmer (2010); Center for Research on Education Outcomes study, Stanford University (2009); Dobbie & Fryer (2009); Farrie & Fine (2010); Finch, Lapsey, & Baker-Boudissa (2009); Gleason, Clark, Tuttle, & Dwoyoer (2010); Grossman & Curran (2004); Hanushek, Kain, & Rivkin (2002); Hoxby, Muraka, & Kang (2009); Kahlenberg (2008); Ladd & Bifulco (2004); Payne & Knowles (2009); Ravitch (2010); Reardon (2009); Robelen (2008); Rogosa (2002); Roy & Mischel (2005); Slovacek, Kunnan, & Kim (2002); Tuttle, Nichols-Barrer, Gill, & Gleason (2010); Wells (2008). |
| **EQUITY** | | |
| To what extent do charters implement equitable admissions policies?<br>Access for English language learners<br>Access for special education students<br>Segregation | Every published study of charter admissions and recruitment documents underenrollment of English language learners and students in special education.<br><br>Studies from Detroit and Minneapolis indicate that charters are more racially segregated than other public schools. | Baker (2010); Buckley & Sattin-Bajaj (2010); Center for Research on Education Outcomes (2009); Communities for Excellent Public Schools (2010a & b); Darling-Hammond (2010); Dingerson, Miner, Peterson, & Walters (2008); Dingerson (2008); Dixon (2009); Farrie & Fine (2010); Frankenberg & Lee (2003); Garcia (2008); de la Torre & Gwynne (2009); Institute on Race and Poverty (2008); Jensen, Kisida, McGee, & Ritter (2010); Lawyers' Committee for Civil Rights Under Law et al. (2010); Mack (2010); Mickelson, Bottia, & Southworth (2008); Otterman (2010); Payne & Knowles (2009); Powell & Frankenberg (2010); Renzulli & Evans (2003); Wells (2008) |

TABLE 3.1. The Promise and the evidence

PARENT ENGAGEMENT

| | | |
|---|---|---|
| Democratic engagement of parents and community | Some individual schools appear to be quite committed to parental engagement. | Communities for Excellent Public Schools (2010a & b); Dingerson, Miner, Peterson, & Walters (2008); Henig (2008); Lipman & Hursh (2007) |
| Parental satisfaction | Some evidence of higher levels of parental satisfaction often diminishing over time. | |
| Parental satisfaction over time | Anecdotal evidence on communities and parents voicing concern of their exclusion from decisions about school closing, charter openings, and charter governance. | |

EXPERIENCE, QUALITY, AND RETENTION OF EDUCATORS

| | | |
|---|---|---|
| Experience and turnover of teachers | Charter educators tend to be less experienced, less qualified, and less well paid than traditional school educators. | Darling-Hammond (2010); Dingerson, Miner, Peterson, & Walters (2008); Henig (2008); Stuit & Smith (2009); Wells (2008) |
| | Charter schools have higher teacher turnover than traditional schools. | |

INNOVATION

| | | |
|---|---|---|
| To what extent do charter schools inspire innovation within traditional local schools? | There has been some writing on innovative practices within exemplary charter schools—but no evidence of widespread curricular or pedagogical innovation across charter school system. | Barr, Sadovnik, & Visconti (2006); Bettinger (2005); Brandon & Weiher (2007); Center for Research on Education Outcomes (2009); Dobbie & Fryer (2009); Payne & Knowles (2009); Zimmer & Buddin (2009) |
| To what extent do charter schools reflect innovative practices? | There has been no systematic analysis of innovation spreading to neighboring public schools, but substantial evidence of charters draining qualified or motivated students and/or families from traditional public schools, educators and families in great intense tension over shared space and limited resources. | |

39

reform, noted, "These scores are dismayingly low . . . . A little more tough love is needed for these schools. Somebody needs to be watching over their shoulders" (Schemo, 2004).

Five years later a national study conducted by the Center for Research on Education Outcomes of Stanford University produced similar findings (2009). CREDO partnered with 15 states and the District of Columbia producing a comprehensive national analysis of charter-school impact on student achievement. The data reveal that charters, in the aggregate, are as effective or less effective than public schools in delivering learning results. More specifically, 17% of charters produce superior outcomes on standardized tests than public schools. However, nearly half of the charter schools nationwide have results that are no different than those of public schools while more than a third (37%) of charters deliver testing results that are significantly worse (Center for Research on Education Outcomes, 2009). More than three-quarters (87%) of charter schools nationally produce the same or worse outcomes than public schools on standardized tests. In an era of evidence and accountability, it seems ironic that these data have not slowed the growth of charter expansion. To the contrary, in the midst of these findings, the growth of charters has accelerated.

A year later, in June 2010, *The Evaluation of Charter School Impacts*, was revised by the U.S. Department of Education, authored by Gleason, Clark, Tuttle, and Dwoyer (of Mathematica Policy Research). The report details a comprehensive analysis of 36 charter middle schools across 15 states, comparing students who applied and were admitted through randomized admissions lotteries to students who applied and were not admitted on a number of outcomes, including academic achievement and satisfaction. As stated in the executive summary, "Students who won lotteries to attend charter schools performed on average no better in mathematics and reading than their peers who lost out in the random admissions process and enrolled in nearby public schools" (Gleason, Clark, Tuttle, & Dwoyer, 2010). The federally commissioned study involved 2,330 students and "represents the first large-scale randomized trial of the effectiveness of charter schools across several states and rural, urban and suburban locales" (Maxwell, 2010)

The study also concludes that the lottery winners did no better on average than the lottery losers on behavior and attendance. While there was substantial variation in impact, there were no differences between lottery winners and lottery losers in outcomes as diverse as absences, suspensions, student effort, student well-being, student behavior and attitudes, and parental involvement. The findings on academic performance echo, in part, those of researchers at Stanford whose 2009 non-randomized multistate study sparked fierce debate.

Once the CREDO and Mathematica studies came to light, President Obama and Secretary of Education Arne Duncan began to stress the policy significance of what they called *high-quality charters.* Duncan reasserted his commitment to charter reform by demanding that unsuccessful charters be closed and successful ones replicated.

> The charter movement is putting itself at risk by allowing too many second-rate and third-rate schools to exist. . . . Charter authorizers need to do a better job of holding schools accountable . . . [we must] get in the business of turning our lowest performing charter schools around. (Dillon, 2009, p. A10)

## From National to Local Evidence

The evidence marshaled nationally by both Mathematica and CREDO is augmented and confirmed by a cross-section of local studies. As suggested by Amy Stuart Wells in a comprehensive review of the charter-impact literature, "Even researchers whose work is more favorable to charter schools and free market reforms reveal only small positive effects for charter school students" (Wells, 2008, p. 172).

We offer brief snapshots of a number of local studies conducted in varied cities and states across the United States to catalogue the patterned impact of charters, despite selectivity in admissions and push-outs. These studies are significant not only because they confirm the national findings but because they frequently offer a more nuanced understanding of achievement outcomes and dynamics associated with charter schooling:

- By early 2006, "only 25 public schools had opened in New Orleans. Eighteen (72%) were charter schools and 10 (40%) had selective admissions standards." By the beginning of the 2007–08 school year, 85 schools had opened and more than half were charter schools. The assessment scores were mixed, demonstrating that, "more charters showed declines in their test scores than improvements" (Dingerson, 2008, p. 32).
- In Newark, New Jersey, Barr, Sadovnik, and Visconti compared the performance of charter and public schools and found that students in charters perform less well on standardized tests than public school students, in particular on language arts tests as compared to mathematics (Barr, Sadovnik, & Visconti, 2006).

- In California, Rogosa found advantages for regular public schools in grades 7 and 8. A more recent report by Margaret Raymond of the Hoover Institute also examines the California experience with charters. Her findings for middle school achievement confirm Rogosa's findings—the performance of public and charter elementary schools is comparable (Rogosa, 2002).
- Eric Bettinger noted that in Michigan, "When charter schools are compared to public schools with similar characteristics pupils in charter schools score no better and may even be doing worse" (Bracey, 2004, p. 19). Randall Eberts and Kevin Hollenbeck "found [that] charter students [in Michigan score] lower by 2–4 percentage points on the MEAP 4th grade reading, 4 percentage points lower on the science testing and 6 percentage points lower on the writing scores" (Bracey, 2005, pp. 19, 43).
- The sixth evaluation of Texas charter schools performed by the Texas Center for Educational Research concluded that "across six school years, traditional public schools have outperformed charter schools. Only 14% of charter schools earned the highest Texas accountability ratings while 86% received the lowest rating" (Bracey, 2004, p. 25).
- In Ohio, the Legislative Office of Education Oversight (LOEO) concluded on the basis of their research that "14 of the 20 comparisons were statistically significant and 13 of those 14 favored traditional public schools."
- The summer of 2010 exposé of New York City "testing fraud" kicked up substantial dirt on the general claims of the Bloomberg-Klein "mayoral control miracle" and, in particular, their claims about charter schools. In terms of charter-traditional school comparisons, the newly determined 2010 cut scores dealt a blow to charter school advocates. As Diane Ravitch suggests in her editorial, "The sounds of bubbles bursting: Student gains on state test vanished into thin air," "The pass rates in the state's charter schools, overall, dropped even faster than those in regular public schools. In third grade math, it plunged from 96.1% to 61.6% and in eighth grade from 84.5% to 50.4%. On the 2010 reading tests, the scores of charter students in New York City were nearly identical to those of district schools: 43% compared to 42%. In math, 63% of the city's charter students passed compared to 54% in public schools" (Ravitch, 2010c).

We turn now to the data on the relationship of cap lifting and quality depletion.

## Lifting Charter Caps and Dropping Achievement

Built into the fabric of Race to the Top is the requirement that states have no legal limit on the number of charters authorized within the jurisdiction. This provision has accelerated a stampede of states "lifting the cap" despite an empirically demonstrated *inverse relationship between rapidly expanding the number of charter schools and the aspiration to lift student testing outcomes.* We review those studies below.

Quite simply, charter performance declines as the number of charter schools increases and oversight capacity grows more lax. This should not be surprising; as the gates are opened more widely, it is difficult to ensure quality control. Deregulation diminishes quality.

Leigh Dingerson (personal communication, February 14, 2011), educational writer and advocate who has studied charter development in a variety of sites, explains that the lifting of charter caps reflects a deep ideological commitment to "letting 1000 flowers bloom, and leav[ing] quality to market forces . . . under the theory that bad ones will close." But, she continues, "The problem is, school closings aren't that easy and parents don't always vote with their feet. It's more complicated than trying out another shoe store."

The question of lifting the cap has been contentious for charter critics and even some advocates. After the release of the CREDO and Mathematica studies and smaller studies documenting the inverse relation of number and quality of charters, some charter advocates expressed concern about a possible reduction in charter quality and oversight in the event of lifting the caps. Ben Lindquist, the executive director of the Charter School Growth Fund, indicated the following:

> Only 6% of the 340 organizations that have sought support have met the organization's academic and financial standards for funding. There just aren't that many charter school operators that are well positioned to expand with quality and efficiency. The risk right now is that we drastically overestimate the capacity of the national charter sector to deliver new high quality seats for underserved families at a sustainable cost to the taxpayer. . . . At this juncture, it is very important not to open the flood gates too wide (through federal funding). If we are not careful we will get a large market segment that is littered with mediocrity. (Lindquist, 2009)

Tom Toch, a leader in the movement for charter reform, recognizes the delicacy of scaling up individual school success, given the complex learning needs of poor inner-city students and the underfunding of charters:

The experience of leading charter management organizations suggests that merely devolving authority to charter school leaders and holding them accountable for results—an approach advocated by many early proponents— is an insufficient reform. (Toch, 2009a, p. 3)

Even Mike Petrilli, vice president for national programs and policy of the Thomas B. Fordham Institute, joined the chorus of cautious advocates when he penned an editorial with a refreshing bit of critical self-reflection on the disappointing impact of the charter school movement on student achievement:

The combination of competitive pressures from below, and accountability pressures from above (were expected to) create a new political environment, one in which unions and civil servants have no real alternative but to accept reform instead of oppose it—out of sheer self-interest. . . . Sounds great, but how has this theory turned out in practice? Not so well. For instance, ten cities boast a charter school "market share" of greater than twenty percent, places like Detroit, Kansas City, and Dayton, which means that their districts have lost loads of kids and cash and teachers. And these districts are also subject to NCLB-style accountability from on high. But to date, their unions and central office staff aren't exactly burning a path to reform's door. (Petrilli, 2010, p. 1)

The twinned dynamic of rapid charter expansion and poor academic performance is illustrated dramatically in the state of Ohio (see Dingerson, 2008). Since 1997, Ohio has been a state with a lax charter law, and prolific expansion and endorsement of charter schools. For academic year 2007–2008, six cities enrolled more than 10% of their students in charter schools. Statewide, over 98% of Ohio school districts subsidize charter schools, some of which are not local. Critics argue that Ohio's charter law "reflects a primary focus on expansion, rather than quality" by permitting private, for-profit corporations to run more than half of the state charter schools; by failing to require community input on charters; by refusing to assess how charter schools impact local public school districts; and by enabling state-level support of for-profit management corporations (p. 7).

Dingerson and colleagues find that Ohio's charter school teachers are less experienced, less qualified, and less well paid than traditional public school educators. The charter schools suffer, further, extremely high rates of teacher turnover. The academic consequences are telling: 65% of the Ohio charters managed by for-profit organizations were placed on the "academic emergency" list, compared to 57% of charters across the state and 12% of traditional schools.

In contrast to Ohio, a number of other states have legislated charter laws that build in quality, community input, and oversight. For instance, Missouri, Kansas, and North Carolina charters must demonstrate their impact on local districts. In Massachusetts, the state reimburses districts partial payment for students lost to charters and caps the amount of money any district can dedicate to charters at 9% (Dingerson, 2008).

## CHARTERS AND THE PROMISE OF EQUITY

We consider here the record on students' equitable access to charters, relying upon three indicators. First, we assess the extent to which charter enrollment reflects the broad demographic diversity of students who attend local public schools. Next we consider the extent to which charters reduce, exacerbate, or are neutral with respect to already existent racial and ethnic segregation in local communities or districts. Third, we review the scant evidence available on charter dropouts, pushouts, and graduation rates.

### Enrollment of English Language Learners and Students in Special Education

Across studies and jurisdictions, evidence consistently suggests that charter schools are less likely than traditional public schools to enroll English language learners and students with learning disabilities (Orfield, 2010, pp. 206, 245, 246). In New York state, 2,627 students in charter schools received special education services in the 2008–2009 school year during a period in which 35,556 students were enrolled. That is, 7.2% of students in charter schools are students with disabilities. On average, charters enroll fewer than half the proportion of special education populations of regular school districts. Equally important, in New York state, 3.8% of students in charters are English language learners compared to 14.2% in district public schools.

Perla Placencia, from the Center for Immigrant Families, told an audience of parents and educators at Medgar Evers College about parent organizing in District 3-Upper West Side and Harlem:

> In Harlem, they are closing schools presumably because of low test scores, and then re-opening charters often not accessible to local students, especially English Language Learners and students enrolled in Special Education. On the Upper West Side, a gentrifying neighborhood, they are closing schools presumably because of test scores and then re-opening with selective criteria to suit the "new" Upper West Side parent. (Placencia, 2010)

As Placencia notes, there is a curious geography to the racialized emergence of charters. To date charters tend to be small schools in urban areas in communities of disproportionate poverty serving largely African-American and Latino youth. However, as of this writing in early 2011, even in New York City we are witnessing the emergence of charters in gentrifying White and elite communities. That said, the charter schools enroll significantly fewer English language learners and students in special education than their local public schools.

## Charters and the Social Stratification of Students

While the Center for Immigrant Families has been tracking charter development and the exclusion of English language learners in Manhattan, the Civil Rights Project at UCLA reports that nearly 80% of Michigan's Black charter-school students attend "intensely segregated minority schools," which are even more segregated than those schools attended by Black children in noncharter Michigan schools (Orfield, 2010). Likewise, the Institute on Race and Poverty finds that in Minnesota,

> Despite nearly two decades of experience, charter schools in Minnesota still perform worse on average than comparable traditional public schools . . . and charter schools have intensified racial and economic segregation in Twin Cities schools. A geographical analysis shows that the racial make-ups of charter schools mimic the racial composition of the neighborhoods where they are located. This contrasts sharply with the claim that charter schools would sever the link between segregated neighborhoods and schools . . . the data show that charter schools are segregating students of color in non-white segregated schools that are even more segregated than the already highly segregated traditional public schools. In some predominantly white urban and suburban neighborhoods, charter schools also serve as outlets for white flight from traditional public schools that are racially more diverse than their feeder neighborhoods. (Institute on Race and Poverty, 2008, p. 1)

Gary Orfield, co-director of the Civil Rights Project at UCLA, conducted a study of 40 states, the District of Columbia, and several dozen metropolitan areas with large enrollments of charters to assess enrollment patterns. Orfield and colleagues conclude that "charters continue to stratify students by race, class, and possibly language and are more racially isolated than traditional public schools in virtually every state and large metropolitan area in the country" (Orfield, 2010, p. 206).

The segregating dynamics provoked and enabled by charters have been investigated by a number of researchers, stated most boldly by Ana

Kiona, a pseudonym used by an educator in a New York City high school in an area being "invaded" by charters catering to the new White elite of the Upper West Side. Kiona ends her "diary of a school designed for closure" with the prophetic question, "Do we see on the horizon the attempt to bring 'charters' back to their origins in the segregation academies of the South?" (Kiona, 2011)

In the aggregate, across states, evidence suggests that charters exacerbate *already existent racial, economic, and ethnic segregation.* But the *forms* of segregation differ. In some states, charters disproportionately enroll low-income youth of color, but in other states charters offer refuge for White-flight (Michelson, et al., 2008; Wells & Roda, 2009). In her review of the empirical studies of charter impact, Wells finds a racially centrifugal pull of charters: "The pattern seems to be that parents are more likely to enroll their children in charter schools with a higher percentage of their own race than nearby public schools" (Wells, 2008, p. 173).

An additional troubling dynamic deserves mention. Research suggests that the charter pull for homogeneity is greatest in those districts that are desegregating. David Garcia confirms that parents choose to leave more racially integrated district schools to attend more racially segregated charters (2008). Renzulli and Evans find that as the level of integration of a community increases, the level of White students enrolling in a predominantly White charter also increases (2003; see also Roy & Mishel, 2005).

It is important to note, however, that these trends toward cultural segregation or specialization are considered desirable in some immigrant communities where local schools are not engaging with culture, language, and diversity as a resource, much less a gift. For example, Camille Jackson, writing in *Teaching Tolerance,* has documented a growing reliance by immigrant parents on specialized charter schools, geared specifically to the needs of distinct immigrant communities (2010).

## Beating the Odds? Or Shaving Off the Poorest of the Poor?

Bruce Baker, a professor at the National Education Policy Center at Rutgers University, published a set of Beating the Odds scatter plots reviewing average performance for New York City public schools and New Jersey schools, based on regression equations accounting for limited-English-proficiency rates, free lunch, mobility, community, and year. The graphs include traditional and charter schools, trying to discern which schools contribute substantially to marked academic gains (as measured by test scores) for marginalized youth. Importantly, Baker finds a few charters among the odds-breakers, but when he does identify a few "high performers" among charters, they tend to underenroll free-lunch students. According to Baker, "New Jersey charter schools in particular are pretty average and those that are better than average serve very few of the lowest income children, no special needs children, and few or no limited English proficient children" (Baker, 2010). Drawing from data across New York and New Jersey, Baker concludes:

> [Charters] seem on average to be taking in the less poor among the poor—at least the "model charters" do. That's simply not scalable reform. Claims by NJ Charter advocates that these schools are serving the same, high poverty, high need student populations as other schools in their neighborhood are simply wrong—and not supported by any legitimate, fine grained analysis. (2010, p. 3)

Baker confirms Gonzalez's prediction about the second tier of public schooling.

## CHARTER SCHOOL DROPOUTS, PUSHOUTS, AND GRADUATION RATES: WHY DO WE KNOW SO LITTLE?

There is surprisingly little known about students' rates of persistence, graduation, dropout, or pushout from charter schools. What is known is largely anecdotal. Charter organizations do not make it easy to access their data. Anecdotes, however, abound.

In the fall 2010, Democrats for Education Reform called a parent meeting in Newark to discuss Race to the Top and charter development in the educational petri dish of Newark, New Jersey. When the conversation turned to charter schools, parents were quite vocal about the rate of pushout they had noticed from charters back to local public schools. Parents took on the school board members: "You ask any administrator, in November, after they get the money, suddenly students start returning to their local high schools from the charters" (Michelle Fine, personal communication, November 2010). A grandmother added, "The charters tell the parents they aren't equipped to handle the child's needs; they can't support special education. They say they don't have the staff to adequately educate these children."

The selective attrition or leakage of charter students back to public schools further concentrates students with the greatest academic and social needs in public schools and segregates motivated survivors in charters. It is no surprise to hear that most seniors in charters are going to college: This is a self-cleansing system. While this dynamic of strategic pushout has not been well documented, anecdotes from across the nation are available—this one from Ohio:

> The Cleveland Academy of Math, Science and Technology closed in November 2003, sending 160 students back to the neighborhood public schools. The founder of the Academy was later convicted of conspiracy, mail fraud and money laundering and sentenced to seven years in prison. (Dingerson, 2008, 34)

Local public schools are of course obligated to readmit students the charter schools find most difficult to educate. Charles Payne has noted, for example, that at KIPP (Knowledge is Power):

> Nearly all students believed that their school would help them get to college. All thought their teachers held high expectations of them. However, there were significant problems, including attrition. Of the students who entered fifth grade in 2003, 60% left before the eighth grade. . . . The portrait here seems to be one of schools having valuable social and academic impacts for a select subgroup of vulnerable children, but not reaching the toughest kids. (Payne & Knowles, 2009, p. 232)

Erick Robelen, a writer for *Education Week,* has investigated KIPP schools, a network of independently run schools that report strong academic achievement increases (Robelen, 2008), as has researcher Gary Miron. The record of KIPP on student attrition is particularly important because of its reputation nationally and internationally as an exemplary charter network. Equally important is the relationship between student exit from KIPP and gains on aggregate testing scores. Miron indicates that there is a 19% drop of test scores in KIPP schools between grades 6 and 7. The scores climb, however, between grades 7 and 8 to 24%.

A study by SRI International also found "high student attrition at the KIPP schools . . . [noting] that lower performing students leave most often. Of the cohort of entering 5th graders at four Bay Area campuses in 2003-2004, a total of 60% had left before the end of 8th grade" (2010).

Holmes Finch, Daniel Lapsley, and Mary Baker-Boudissa confirm high rates of student mobility away from charter schools (2009). In particular, students with higher initial achievement scores, those living in poverty, and those who were "non Caucasian" were more likely to exit the charter school prematurely. In addition, schools with less experienced faculty had higher early departure rates than schools with more experienced faculty.

Reviews of the Harmony Schools, a nonprofit network of charters operating in Texas, have generally been positive regarding test scores and student achievement. Recently, however, *USA Today* reported that parents have accused one Harmony school of removing or counseling out underperforming students. This specific practice in a single school was generalized by Ed Fuller, a University of Texas researcher, on the basis of his findings on Harmony Schools throughout the state. He indicated that the network has an extraordinarily high student attrition rate of about 50% for students in grades 6 through 8 (Toppo, 2010).

In an analysis of the much-acclaimed SEED school in Washington, DC, featured in the film *Waiting for Superman*, Zein El-Amine and Lee Glazer report significant levels of expulsions, suspensions, and students who are held back and then withdraw:

> Although SEED sends its graduates to college, it has  significant rates of expulsions and suspensions, and its practice of often retaining students at the lower grades results in a high rate of voluntary withdrawal. The school maintains an entering class of 40 students, but has never graduated more than 21 in a year. In 2007, only 12 students graduated. (El-Amine & Glazer, 2008, p. 55)

While these small studies or case studies point in a consistent direction and are confirmed by anecdote, interestingly there are no systematic studies that estimate a reliable dropout rate for charter schools. Perhaps this is because no one has studied charter-school attrition or because it is quite difficult to distinguish dropouts from those students who are simply asked to leave or choose to leave their charters and return to traditional public schools. Like a slow and selective leak, the charter-attrition students presumably return to the public schools. They are not  documented as dropouts, as they would be if they left a traditional school.

Dingerson (personal communication, January 2011) points to another strategy by which charter enrollment fluctuates and children are asked to leave. She writes, "Virtually all charter schools require parents and students to sign a 'contract' upon enrollment. The contracts typically require parents to offer some number of hours volunteering for the school (often it appears turning out to represent the charter movement at various hearings counts toward volunteer time), [or the schools] might require parents to read to their child for a period of time each night, and or require students to maintain a certain grade point average." While Dingerson recognizes some of these contractual obligations may also be in place in public schools, and may even be educationally beneficial, she reports that some charters use parents refusal to sign a

TABLE 3.2. New Jersey Charter Persistence and Attrition

| Category | 9th grade 2006–2007 | 10th grade 2007–2008 | 11th grade 2008-2009 | 12th grade 2009–2010 |
|---|---|---|---|---|
| Charter schools | 748 | 679 | 651 | 619 (83%) |
| All schools statewide | 104,145 | 98,861 | 93,9990 | 91,360 (88%) |

*Source*: Data provided by the New Jersey Department of Education, 2010, Fall Survey Enrollments; analysis conducted by Education Law Center, Fall 2010, Newark, New Jersey.

contract as a reason to deny admission, or parents' noncompliance with the contract as the basis for what they euphemistically call "voluntary withdrawal" hearings to push kids out. At the initial point of contact, the charter school will press parents hard about whether or not the parents can meet the terms of the contract, suggesting that parents look elsewhere if they have doubts.

Thus, with subtlety and bold action, charters are much more likely (and able) to selectively admit, maintain and remove students. Local public schools have to pick up the pieces. So let's turn to the data and see how well charters in New Jersey fare, even with these fluctuations in enrollment.

## A Quick Look at New Jersey Charter Data

As noted above, it is difficult to specify charter dropout/pushout rates because data systems do not, for the most part, report individual student progress over time. With publicly available New Jersey Department of Education data, and the research staff at the Education Law Center, we were able to estimate a Charter Attrition Rate for the secondary charter schools in New Jersey by tracking the entering ninth grade for 2006–2007 through to the graduating twelfth grade in 2009–2010, by comparing the size of the incoming ninth grade with the size of the outgoing twelfth grade 4 years later. With such a cohort comparison, one can at least determine charter leakage, although it is unknown what percentage of the graduating twelfth graders actually started at that school 4 years prior.

The official New Jersey secondary charter dropout rate is listed as 1.2% (compared with 1.5% for the state) and the cohort persistence rate is calculated at 83%. However, as Table 3.2 reflects, the student body fluctuation rate is substantial—at least 17% over 4 years and undoubtedly higher given that we do not know how many of the twelfth graders started in the ninth grade 4 years prior. Further, as Table 3.3 reflects, the

TABLE 3.3. Fluctuations in Charter Enrollment Over Time: Ninth-Grade Class
Size (2006–2007) to Twelfth-Grade Class Size (2009–2010)

| Charter School* | 9th Grade | 10th Grade | 11th Grade | 12th Grade |
|---|---|---|---|---|
| Brown Charter | 55 | 50 | 60 | 45 |
| Red Charter | 122 | 110 | 93 | 86 |
| Blue Charter | 127 | 68 | 65 | 67 |
| Green Charter | 49 | 50 | 41 | 62 |

*Pseudonyms are used representing charters distributed across the state.

variation in class size across years (displaying a selection of four charters from across the state) reflects substantial movement of student bodies into and out of charter schools.

Reviewing the full archive of materials available on New Jersey secondary charters in terms of test performance and student attrition, the scant evidence available suggests that students attending charter schools in New Jersey score on a par with students from the lowest-income/worst-performing district in the state.

This is true even though a number of the charter students are not from the poorest districts and charters selectively admit and retain fewer students in need of special-education services and fewer English language learners than peer schools.

## THE EFFECT OF CHARTERS ON PARENT INVOLVEMENT

For decades, education scholars including James Comer, Joyce Epstein, Annette Lareau, Angela Valenzuela, and Jeannie Oakes have argued that school performance and individual student achievement are intimately bound up with family involvement in the education process, both inside and outside the school building. Clearly, such involvement has too frequently been unwelcome in public schools and sometimes overtly resisted by many teachers and principals.

While there have been many concerns that local parents and communities have been absented from the charter-planning process, evidence suggests relatively high rates of family satisfaction with charters. Henig cites a number of studies indicating that families of charter school students are more satisfied with charter schools than comparable samples of parents of traditional school children and that they are more satisfied than they were with the schools they exited (Henig, 2008). However, in a study of charter-parent satisfaction over time, Buckley and Schneider surveyed families over four waves and found that the "charter school advantage in parental satisfaction . . . declined over time and virtually disappeared by the end of five years" (as cited in Henig, 2008, p. 118).

In most states, parents and communities have been shut out of the democratic process of creating or governing charter schools. Unlike their public counterparts, charter boards do not have a legal obligation to hold collective meetings with parents or local communities to discuss areas of policy-practice agreement or difference. Even democratic forums as politically benign as parent associations have been difficult to establish in charter schools. A recent controversy in New York state crystallizes the issue. Advocates for parent associations see it as an issue of principle and/or parents' rights. Those who oppose parent associations have indicated that a single authority to enforce such policy does not exist and that charter schools are supposed to be free of such mandates (Otterman, 2010). One parent powerfully articulated her frustration with the apparent contradictory stance of the charter movement: "They want us to be in Albany to lobby and talk from a script about equal funding and raising the cap. . . . What about other things? If they really want to involve parents they have nothing to fear" (Otterman, 2010).

This marginalization of collective voice and minimization of democratic practice has significant implications regarding the relationship of parents to their schools. The loss of voice as a result of both public officials' rush to charter reform and charter schools' greater insulation from parents is illustrated by a letter written by New York State Assemblyman Daniel O'Donnell to Chancellor Joel Klein in response to the decision of the New York state Department of Education to move the Harlem Success Charter into the building of Middle School 241.

> I write to express my outrage at the disrespect exhibited yesterday in its handling of the proposal to house Harlem Success Academy at M241. . . . Yesterday's treatment of the parents and leaders of District 3 completely refutes any assertion by DOE that it wishes to meaningfully involve parents in decision making at any level. I have learned that no advance notice was given to the public, parents, leaders, or District 3 staff. . . . I also learned that charter school had time to arrange for two busloads of advocates to attend and testify and outfit their speakers with the school's apparel. Yesterday's true message could not be clearer: DOE has made its decision about PS 241's future and will proceed regardless of the hearings outcome. No other meaning could be derived from failing to give notice of a public hearing or from the brief, inconvenient window during which stakeholders could sign up to testify. (O'Donnell, 2009)

## THE PROMISE OF CHARTER INNOVATION
## AS A PATHWAY TO IMPROVING PUBLIC EDUCATION

Charles Payne, sociologist of education, has been studying charters and more traditional public schools in Chicago, documenting what he calls the promise and perils of both. He notes that some charters indeed offer new schooling options for children and are a potential magnet for developing relatively robust institutional partnerships and stakeholder relationships to educational outcomes for the poorest students. He suggests that perhaps the most compelling strength of charters lies in their flexibility to innovate. This flexibility is generally understood as a counterpoint to the often inflexible or rigid bureaucratic practices of public education that have straight-jacketed much of the transformative potential of schooling. This flexibility has a number of forms, including (1) ability to hire staff with minimal restrictions and to fire staff who do not perform, (2) capacity to extend the school day and year, (3) budgetary autonomy to make those investments most likely to yield improved academic performance, (4) testing of new governance methods or designs to maximize "teacher and parent voice and deepen civic engagement with the purposes of the school," and (5) insulation of charters from district policies, thus freeing staff from the escalating time and resource demands associated with district mandates and compliance (Payne & Knowles, 2009, pp. 228–229). Implicit in this analysis is the belief that freedom from bureaucratic rules and parts of union contracts will foster the innovation necessary to improve academic achievement and that the accretion of the lessons learned from charter successes will be used by policy makers and educators to improve public education overall (Payne & Knowles, 2009).

Indeed, and perhaps ironically, charter schools have been granted the very freedoms that small-school educators, progressive educators, and reformers have been requesting for decades. There is, of course, a bitter irony apparent—charters have been granted the very flexibility that progressive public schools have long sought and been denied (see Cook & Tashlik, 2005b).

But Payne and Knowles also recognize the limits of school-by-school reform:

> When the stars are in alignment, charters give us a means to do an end run on . . . incompetent bureaucracies and give some children a better education. . . . But this does not mean that charters are a panacea for the ills of urban systems writ large. (2009, pp. 231–232)

Given that some exemplary charters are deeply innovative, to what extent can or does this form of innovation migrate to local traditional schools? Thus, we investigate below the hypothesis of innovation contagion, particularly in intimate settings of co-location.

## The Hypothesis of Innovation-Contagion

Early in the charter movement there was a claim that charters would spur innovation in the larger public-education system; that there would be a contagion effect, so to speak. To the question of innovation-contagion, there is no database that collects information on charter school practices their dissemination in public schools. Instead, intensified competition regarding test scores reduces charter schools' interest in sharing effective practices with other public schools. Clearly, exceptions to this trend do exist. For example, in Newark, New Jersey, there has been an attempt to bring together principals from charters and traditional public schools to discuss the most effective practices. The degree to which these meetings are sustained or produce a concrete yield that benefits public schools has yet to be determined.

The hypothesis of innovation-contagion needs to be analyzed on three counts. First, do charters in the aggregate, not just exemplars, actually embody innovation? Second, is it the case that existent public schools are not innovative? Third, what is the presumed mechanism by which charters are supposed to inspire local public schools to innovate?

## The Effect of Charters on Traditional Schools' Performance

To the question, does charter school competition improve the performance of traditional public schools? The evidence is not very compelling. A California-based study by Zimmer and Buddin compared traditional- and charter school outcomes in the same communities and found that traditional public school principals reported little competitive pressure from charters. Further, the student achievement analysis fails to demonstrate that charter competition provokes improved performance of traditional public schools (2009).

Lee investigated a similar question in Michigan and found no statistically significant improvement in district levels of efficiency or achievement (2009). Ni, drawing on the same Michigan data set, found that charter competition depressed student achievement and school efficiency in Michigan's traditional public schools. The effect was small initially and then more substantial over time (2009).

Brandon and Weiher investigated this question in Texas, by comparing "peer group" schools that were close to charters and more distant traditional schools, on four outcomes: test performance, graduation rates, dropout rates, and attendance rates (2007). The authors find that "competition schools show no greater improvement on these outcomes than schools that did not experience competition" (p. 1).

Bettinger's 2005 study of charter schools in Michigan compared to local schools is often cited as the most rigorous test of innovation-contagion. Bettinger found no effect of charter schools on test scores in public schools within 5 miles. Wellesley economist Patrick McEwan confirms these findings nationally:

> The statistical analysis suggests that increasing competition has no significant impact on math test scores, but it has small positive effects on language scores. The report does not conclusively demonstrate that the results are explained by increasing competitive pressure on public school administrators; they may also be explained by shifting peer quality or declining short run class sizes in public schools. (as cited in Baker, 2010, p. 2)

### Just Ask the Janitor:
### How Shared Space Breeds Contempt, Not Innovation

One might suspect that the hypothesis of innovation contagion would best be tested in co-location situations in which charters and traditional schools share space. And yet, emergent evidence suggests just the opposite. The ever-greater competition between public schools and charters over an essentially fixed pot of resources—particularly real estate, motivated students/families, and money—has produced bitter squabbling in many cities. New York City, for example, has become the cautionary tale for charter public school co-location, that is, placing charter schools in the same buildings with traditional public schools. Some part of the rationale for co-location was the rather oblique assumption that proximity would advantage public schools by maximizing probability of transmission of innovative practices from charters to neighborhood schools. Such promises, however, have not been realized. Rather, co-location has produced zero sum competition for scarce resources. This intensifying competition involves increasingly more public school buildings in New York City and produces escalating political conflict.

More than two-thirds of charter schools in New York City in 2010 were located in public school buildings, yielding an estimated savings of $2,712 per student for those charter schools (see New York City Independent Budget Office Fiscal Brief, 2010). Arguments over space, privilege, quality of the facility, cleanliness, and janitorial responsibilities, however, have been quite publicly aired in the media and in the hallways of schools. One parent from a traditional school, which is now co-located in the same building as a charter, complains that the charter is taking over coveted space and educational opportunities previously available to the traditional school students.

> "It's not fair to our students," she said of the decision, which gives the char-ter students access to the room for most of the day. "It's depriving them of a fully functioning library, something they deserve . . ." Even determining how many rooms are free is contentious—most schools use open space for activi-ties, dance, computers, and tutoring—but the Education Department officials come in and treat those rooms as "underutilized space" to allow for another school to come in. (Medina, 2009a, p. 1)

In some cases, as in Harlem and Brownsville, the regular public school has not performed well and has seen enrollments shrink while parents flock to the charter on the other side of the building. Char-ter schools that have had success raising private donations have new desks and computers to show for it. And most charter school teaching staffs are not unionized, giving them vastly different work rules and pay scales.

Parents and community members blasted former city councilwoman Eva Moskowitz, head of Harlem Success Academies, for using what they call unfair influence, citing emails between her and Klein, first published in the *Daily News* last month:

> "I am not against charter schools. I'm against charter schools that bully their way into public schools at the expense of our children," said Assemblyman Keith Wright (D-Harlem). Wright joined parents and community members at a rally outside Public School 123 on W. 140th St., which shares its build-ing with one of Moskowitz's Harlem Success Academies. E-mails between the pair of school officials show Moskowitz had direct access to Klein. At Moskowitz's request, Klein attended fund-raisers, helped her land a $1 mil-lion donation, and intervened on her behalf in clashes with subordinates, the e-mails show. Advocates say the "unfair" relationship is disturbing and hurts Harlem's children. "They have a cozy relationship that goes back as far as 2007," said William Hargraves, parent of a Public School 123 graduate. "She targeted certain schools . . . She seems to have a magic wand to get whatever she wants." Moskowitz did not respond to a request for comment and has said it's her job to advocate for her schools and that she did nothing wrong. "I don't just quietly accept what is dished out to our parents and what I believe are unfair allocations of space that hurt my schools," she said last month. (Goldsmith, 2010)

The difficulties that charters face in financing new school construction have resulted in a troubling redistribution of public school space to charters. Space, monies, media attention, public policy, and academically motivated students/families flow in one direction while an ideological attack on public schools, teachers, and unions flows back like refuse in the undertow.

## TEACHER EXPERIENCE AND STABILITY
## AS PREDICATES FOR INNOVATION

A central argument of Linda Darling-Hammond's book, *The Flat World and Education* (2010a), holds that to educate effectively and inventively requires a stable teaching and leadership cohort. The U.S. Department of Education National Center on Education Statistics in 2008 reported that 38% of charter school teachers have 4 or fewer years of experience compared to 18% of the teachers in public schools. Low experience, low quality, and high turnover of teachers and principals adversely affect school culture, classroom innovation, teaching, and learning.

To this question, evidence suggests that teachers in many charter schools and networks are less experienced and relatively inexpensive when compared to public school colleagues, and they put in longer hours working in very demanding environments. In KIPP charter schools, for example, teachers work an average of 65 hours per week, 25% longer than teachers in public schools (Toch, 2009b, p. 19). Small pay-differentials and bonuses in charter schools have not made a difference in the retention or performance of teachers, as evidenced by both aggregated academic performance of students and teacher turnover rates.

Examples of relatively high teacher turnover in charter networks are abundant. For example, the KIPP network has suffered in Houston and the Bay Area from very high teacher turnover (Toch, 2009a, p. 35). The retention rates of teachers at KIPP and Yes Prep in Houston were reported by journalists to be far higher than in the public schools (p. 35). Both schools have a disproportionate number of young and inexperienced teachers. The constant leakage of adults and students is a worrisome feature of these schools. For-profit charter networks, like the Edison Schools, have abandoned parts of their increasingly demanding work environments because of teacher opposition. When Philadelphia transitioned to charter schools in 2003, data indicated that the long-standing problem of retaining teachers and attracting fully certified teachers intensified.

A large part of the teaching work force for charters is provided by Teach for America (TFA). Toch indicates that TFA anticipates supplying 3,600 new teachers in the fall of 2010 and 8,000 by 2015. These teachers are drawn from an impressive pool of young, able graduates from a cross-section of the best schools in America. Importantly, however, TFA graduates represent both an opportunity and a challenge for charter schools and, more largely, public education. Unsurprisingly, many of the recruits from TFA see teaching as a transitional post-graduation job rather than a long-term career. These issues are compounded for charters by the difficulty of finding a sufficient pool of talented teachers outside of major cities (Toch, 2009a, p. 21). The problem of recruiting and retaining teachers is a long-standing problem for both public and charter schools. The vulnerability of inexperienced instructors to burnout and exit is especially high in charters and, in turn, often undermines the possibility for experimentation (Fruchter, 2007, p. 93).

In general, to the extent that evidence is available, it appears that charters have had a difficult time recruiting and retaining teachers because of their relatively low salaries and greater work demand. The KIPP foundation director noted in early 2009 that on a scale of 1 to 10, they were at 2 in developing and retaining teachers. The recruitment dilemma—if not the retention problem—may be finding a perverse solution in the hemorrhaging of educators from public schools caused by massive layoffs. For instance, the 2008–2009, 2009–2010, and upcoming 2010 waves of layoffs that occurred and would occur in cities like Los Angeles have increased the flow of educators into the charter system and out of the traditional public school system. Another version of flooding the zone.

To the extent that data are available, evidence suggests that the charter school work force is a bit more unstable and inexperienced than its public counterparts. While the difference is modest, the reality departs dramatically from the promise of highly innovative, stable schools for children of poverty.

## SUMMARY

A systematic review of the evidence on charter impact suggests great variation among the charter sector. In the aggregate, an analysis of the available empirical material on the academic accomplishments of charters suggests the following:

- *Achievement.* Charter student achievement levels are in the main comparable to, and often below, traditional schools.
- *Lifting the charter cap and achievement.* The more charters in a state, the more varied—and worse—are the overall achievement data.
- *Equity.* The charter sector enrolls disproportionately few students with special needs and English language learners. The admissions

and pushout strategies of charter schools exacerbate already high levels of race/ethnic/class educational segregation. These schools suffer high rates of attrition and, therefore, produce high rates of college going among students who graduate.

- *Teacher quality and turnover.* Charters tend to employ younger, cheaper, and less experienced educators with high turnover-rates.
- *Parent satisfaction.* Charters cultivate, at least initially, relatively high rates of parental satisfaction that wane, however, over time. Former charter parents whose children have been returned to traditional public schools, however, tend not to report high satisfaction ratings.
- *Innovation.* While some charters appear to take advantage of their freedoms and thereby engage in innovative teaching and learning practices, others enforce quite rigid teaching and learning practices.
- *Innovation-contagion.* There is no evidence of innovation-contagion spread through the public sector. To the contrary, in shared space, there are often conflicts and dramatic displays of inequitable distribution of resources and opportunities.

Turning to the external consequences of the charter sector on the larger local community and public school system, the evidence points to four conclusions:

- *Parents.* Parents and local community leaders as democratic collectives have been excluded from decision making about and governance of charters.
- *Students.* Most children in low-income communities have been left behind in the proliferation of charters. Particularly neglected and abandoned are the disproportionate population of high-needs students in the public sector.
- *Educators.* Senior educators as professionals with experience, skill, and craft have been replaced by short-term, often well-educated but inexperienced, young teachers who typically do not stay in charters for many years. Thus, the level of skill and professionalism of the teaching profession is rapidly declining.
- *Local democratic practice.* Community voice and engagement in public affairs shrinks as public school accountability shifts out of the local neighborhood to networks of for-profits or even non-profits.

# CHAPTER 4

# Interlocking Power and the Deregulation of Public Education

A dominant assumption of every economically advanced nation is that social policy development works in tandem with the rigorous collection, sifting, and synthesis of data enabling best strategic investment decisions with finite resources. What the prior chapter makes very clear, however, is that evidence has simply not informed charter school policy. To the contrary, we know from multiple data sets that public schools are modestly outperforming charters. This pattern is in place over an approximate 10-year period and has been documented through national evaluations and studies on the performance of charters in a cross-section of states. In a rational world where evidence drives policy, charter school momentum would have been slowed if not halted years ago. What, then, explains the discordance between policy and evidence?

It is important to note that policy making has never been purely incubated out of evidence-based social laboratories. Rather, economic gain, political power, and social tumult offer three other frames for explaining the emergence of policies as varied as Social Security, Section 8 housing, and banking regulation. However, evidence or data has generally played a critical role in helping to shape the state's strategic policy decision making within these highly politicized and often socially charged environments. The influence of evidence in shaping policy, however, has declined precipitously as the boundary between corporate influence and state autonomy has disappeared. The ever-greater emphasis on deregulating state functions emerges out of a 30-year political tide that has washed away many government functions. Cascading corporate and individual wealth dedicated to specific political campaigns has been the sharp instrument allowing dominant economic interests to both compromise and penetrate the strategic functions of the state.

## THE INFLUENCE OF WEALTH ON PUBLIC POLICY

Even more concretely, this wealth has been dedicated to reshaping political discourse and the outcome of elections to ensure the implementation of policies that promise specific benefits. These benefits largely accrue from two policies—the deregulation and privatization of government functions. The former policy allows corporate and private interests to shed costly government accountability, ranging from environmental to banking regulation. The privatization of government functions is the policy du jour of ever more deregulated environments interested in creating marketplace alternatives and capitalizing a range of government services. It is within this context that charter-school policy has gained traction despite what otherwise might have been the impediment of a very slight record of academic success. Christopher Hedges and Diane Ravitch have described the social environment that drives state deregulation in these two quotes:

> Over the past few decades, we have watched the rise of a powerful web of interlocking corporate entities, a network of arrangements within sub-sectors, industries, or other partial jurisdictions to diminish and often abolish outside control and oversight. These corporations have neutralized national, state, and judicial authority. The corporate state, begun under Ronald Reagan . . . has destroyed the public and private institutions that protected and safeguarded citizens. (Hedges, 2009, p. 169)

> Regardless of competing research studies, the charter school sector continued to expand rapidly, as states and districts turned to private agencies and entrepreneurs to solve the problems of education. As more charter schools opened, advocacy for charters in Washington and state capitals grew stronger, supported by major foundations. . . . Everyone knew the charter sector was big, bold, diverse, and getting bigger, bolder, and more diverse. Their quality ranged from excellent to awful. That's what happens when an industry is deregulated and the sluice gates are opened to release a huge flow of innovation, entrepreneurship, and enterprise. So, ironically at the very time that the financial markets were collapsing and as deregulation of financial markets got a bad name, many of the leading voices in American education assured the public that the way to educational rejuvenation was through deregulation. (Ravitch, 2010a, p. 144)

Legitimating the deregulation of government functions such as public schooling is largely achieved through the discourse of a naturalized ideological truth about the effectiveness of market reform. On this basis, many business leaders, politicians, and foundations argue that the deregulation and privatization of education is the only alternative to the encrusted and ineffective work of the bureaucratic systems of public schooling. Increasingly, deregulation and the creative-destructive market forces it unleashes are the new dictum for public education. Critical to this discussion, charter schools are viewed as the organizational instrument expected to transform a deregulated public education marketplace into an engine for academic achievement. Importantly, this ideological motive is not isolated or unadulterated. Rather it rotates in a gravitational relationship to an interlocking constellation of political, economic, and ideological interests and forces.

As Trip Gabriel of *The New York Times* described, the intersection between foundation, business, political, and charter leadership has taken on the quality of the "cool kids'" table:

> In the world of education, it was the equivalent of the cool kids' table in the cafeteria. Executives from the Bill and Melinda Gates Foundation, McKinsey Consultants, and scholars from Stanford and Harvard met at the New Schools Venture Fund in Pasadena, California . . . . Many of those at the meeting last May had worried that the Obama administration would reflect the general hostility of teachers unions toward charters. . . . But all doubts were dispelled when the image of Arne Duncan filled a large video screen and pledged to combine "your ideas with your dollars from the federal government. What you have created" he said, is "a real movement." (Gabriel & Medina, 2010, p. A1)

Philanthropists have been joined by investment bankers at the charter support events:

> Wall Street has always put its money where its interests and beliefs lie. But it is far less common that so many financial heavyweights would adopt a social cause like charter schools and advance it with laser like focus in the political realm. Although the April 9th breakfast with Andrew Cuomo was not a formal fundraiser, the hedge fund managers have been wielding their money to influence educational policy in Albany, particularly among Democrats . . . historically aligned with the teachers union. The money paid for television and radio advertisements, phone banks, and 40 canvassers in NYC and Buffalo—all urging voters to . . . "raise the maximum number of charters from 200 to 460." (Gabriel & Medina, 2010, p. A1)

## THE STATE AND PHILANTHROPY

Diane Ravitch argues that the very future of public education is being undermined by the rapid proliferation and misplaced faith in charters—a faith that, Ravitch argues, can be traced to a leading edge of investment and political legitimacy offered by corporate and foundation decision makers:

> The "Billionaires Boys Club" is a discussion of how we are in a new era of the foundations and their relationship to education. We have never in our history of the United States had foundations with the wealth of the Gates Foundations and some of the other billionaire foundations—the Walton Foundation, the Broad Foundation. And these three foundations—Gates, Broad, and Walton—are committed now to charter schools and evaluating teachers by test scores. And now that's the policy of the U.S. Department of Education. We have never had anything like this, where foundations have the ambition to direct national education policy and are in fact succeeding. (Ravitch, *Democracy Now* interview, March 5, 2010c)

Clearly, the interlocking interests of political and business leadership are not confined to local or city decision making. For example, federal-policy-making circles include a number of key Gates Foundation officials.

The fact that former Gates Foundation officials are working for the Department of Education is not independently significant. The evidence, however, of the interpenetration of Gates money and Department of Education policy, however, is noteworthy. To begin with, the deputy secretary of the Department of Education, James Shelton, and Secretary of Education Duncan's chief of staff, Margot Rogers, "came from the foundation and were granted waivers by the administration from its revolving door policy limiting involvement with former employees" (Golden, 2010, p. 62). The dynamic interplay between present and former Gates Foundation officials and the federal reform agenda is clear.

What distinguished the Gates Foundation from other foundations such as Soros and Ford, which also share an interest in public education reform, is the amount of money at its disposal and the strategic dedication of its powerful social network and economic resources to advance a narrow band of public policies. To date, the foundation has had an extraordinary influence on the making of federal public education policy. At the center of its agenda is charter reform.

The Gates Foundation's influence is felt in a number of ways. For example, the day before the presidential debate in 2007, both Gates and Broad announced that they would jointly fund a $60 million campaign to influence both political parties to promote the foundations' "version of educational reform" (Barkan, 2011, p. 6). This investment represents perhaps the single most expensive attempt to influence public policy. By way of comparison, it dwarfed the $7.8 million  campaign waged by AARP to influence policy related to elderly issues in the same year (Barkan,

2011). After Barack Obama was elected president, the Gates Foundation intensified its efforts to influence federal education policy. One example of Gates's effort to advance its reform agenda is its publication of *The Turnaround Challenge*, "the authoritative how to guide on turnaround. Secretary of Education Arne Duncan has called it 'the bible' for school restructuring. He has incorporated it into federal policy, and reformers around the country use it. . . . The document has been downloaded 200,000 times since 2007" (Barkan, 2011, p. 6).

The Gates Foundation is not alone in its policy commitment to the expansion of charter schools. There is a shared understanding among a cross-section of very powerful foundation, political, and business actors that charter reform in a deregulated public education environment is the mechanism of choice for transforming schooling. Choice and competition are seen as the singular policy option for the regeneration of public schools.

It is within this context that a cross-section of foundations with close ties to business interests have helped to spearhead and enlarge charter reform by extending financial support to targeted schools. This point was amplified by Tom Toch when he noted that new foundations sympathetic to entrepreneurial school reform were entering education (Toch, 2009b). As noted, the Bill and Melinda Gates Foundation embraced CMOs in its pursuit of alternatives to dysfunctional school systems. In addition, the Walton family foundation, a creation of the WalMart empire, saw charter networks as a way of expanding its commitment to school choice. The Walton and Gates foundations were joined by three other foundations established by wealthy entrepreneurs: The Doris and Donald Fisher Fund, founders of the Gap, The Eli and Edythe Broad Foundation, founded with money from homebuilding, and the Michael and Susan Dell Foundation, funded by Dell's computer fortune (Toch, 2009b, p. 4).

The mission of the Broad Foundation is to transform urban public education through better governance, management, labor relations, and competition. In addition, as noted on its website, the foundation's intention is to advance entrepreneurship for the public good in education. The Broad Foundation has also invested in a residency program "which places professionals with master's degrees and several years into full time managerial positions in school districts, charter-school management organizations and state as well as federal government education departments" (Barkan, 2011, p. 3). The strategic implications of investing in pipelines as contrasted with programs are significant. Frederick Hess, the director of the Education Policies Studies Institute, located at the conservative American Enterprise Institute, suggests that pipeline investment represents an opportunity to more effectively and indirectly implement their reform agenda:

Donors have continual choice between supporting "programs" or supporting "pipelines." Programs which are common are ventures that directly involve a limited population of children and educators. Pipelines, on the other hand primarily seek to attract new talent to education, keep those individuals engaged, or create new opportunities for talented practitioners to advance and influence the profession . . . By seeking to alter the composition of the educational workforce, pipelines offer foundations a way to pursue a high leverage strategy . . . [for reform]. (Barkan, 2011, p. 4)

Consistent with Tom Toch's perspective, the Broad Foundation indicates that entrepreneurial reformers in tight alignment with the "creative forces of the market" are a best hope for transforming public education (Broad Foundation website). These layers of interlocking power have dedicated a substantial part of their economic and political capital to building a charter movement. This investment is intended to create the political and policy momentum to expand charter schools and, thus, improve and ultimately replace public education no matter the evidence.

## THE CHARTER CAMPAIGN AND POLITICAL MOBILIZATION OF THE PRIVATE SECTOR: THE CASE OF NEW YORK STATE

The intimate relationship between the influence of patron giving, the growing legitimacy of the charter movement, and an increasing commitment across the electoral-political spectrum to deregulate public schooling are powerfully embedded features of educational policy-making, most apparent in New York state. A vivid example is the relationship between former Governor David Paterson's recent support to double the charter school cap and a cross-section of major contributors to his campaign with a significant stake in such reform. Five donors, who in total contributed about $250,000, are former or present board members of the right-wing think tank the Manhattan Institute and stalwart advocates for charter reform. Another donor, J. C. Huzienga, who contributed $20,000, is president of the for-profit National Heritage Academies Incorporated, which runs four charters in New York City. Its website recently indicated that the network has "staked out a solid claim in the still evolving field of for profit K–8 education (New York State United Teachers [NYSUT], 2009). Finally, the most significant contributor is the widow of WalMart heir John Walton, who donated almost $60,000 to Paterson's political campaign. The commitment of the Walton Foundation to charter reform and more largely right-wing causes is long established. A concise summary of their involvement nationally and in New York state is provided below:

> Donations from the Walton Family in New York include a 10 million dollar construction loan from the Wal-Mart family's foundation to the Brighter Choice Foundation as well as generous support for many individual charter schools. While the Brighter Choice schools receive the lions share of philanthropic support, the Walton Family in recent years, also donated 199,000 dollars to the Bronx Charter School for Excellence; 155,000 dollars to the Central New York Charter Schools; 215,000 dollars for the Western New York Maritime Charter Schools, and 200,000 dollars to the Bronx Charter School for Children. (NYSUT, 2010a, p. 4)

A number of the most influential agency advocates in New York state for charter reform, including the Charter Resource Center, School Choice Scholarships Foundation, the Foundation for Education Reform and Accountability (FERA), and the Brighter Choice Foundation, largely draw their funding from the same small number of groups and share a space. This intersection of space and purpose led one group to declare that they promote the appearance that they are separate organizations representing separate interests. In fact, they are essentially one powerful and influential organization. Importantly, this was the historic headquarters of Change-NY, a statewide group advocating a range of right-wing policy initiatives including charter reform. The connection between Change-NY, conservative foundation giving, and charter reform is illustrated below:

> Other foundations also give heavily to support and expand charter schools in New York. They include the Hickory Foundation (Virginia Manheimer of Change-NY); the Gilder Foundation (Richard Gilder, of Change-NY); Kovner Foundation (run by Bruce Kovner, a hedge fund operator and close friend of VP Dick Cheney); and the Bradley Foundation (Lynde and Harry Bradley of Milwaukee; gives heavily to pro-voucher initiatives and school choice campaigns as well as charter schools nationwide), along with the Robert W. Wilson Trust and Simon Foundation. Financier Carl Icahn also gives heavily. (NYSUT, 2010c, pp. 3–5)

Clearly, there is a powerful intersection between money, electoral politics, and charter reform. This architecture of shared interest is underpinned by foundation expertise and grant-giving, legitimating and financing charter reform. Simultaneously, wealthy individuals often affiliated with these foundations have supported the campaigns of politicians sympathetic to the continued deregulation of public education or the expansion of charter schooling. As noted, these political dynamics are, in part, driven by marketplace ideology regarding deregulation. An equally powerful factor lubricating deregulation of charter schooling is economic incentives.

## CHARTER SCHOOLS AND THE MAXIMIZATION
## OF ECONOMIC GAIN:
## PROFITING FROM THE PRIVATIZATION OF PUBLIC SCHOOLS

As the New York example reflects, the motives of charter reformers are not easily reduced to a single variable, for instance, economic gain. Importantly, ideological predisposition and/or belief in business principles are motives also driving charter reform. Equally important, many charter advocates including hedge-fund managers are interested in supporting ventures that in their estimation maximize the probability of improvement in the academic performance of very poor youngsters. More to the point, a small but significant number of the engaged philanthropists have grown up in very poor communities and bring into the work a difficult history with public education and schools overwrought with local, often corrupt, politics. They understand that many of the public schools in their neighborhood did not work for their friends and relatives. By dint of hard work, intelligence, and good luck, they made it. With a sincere commitment to improve the chances of the next generation of youngsters, they are betting on charter schooling as an option for a segment of youngsters from communities similar to the ones in which they were raised.

At the same time, in a period of profound economic instability, the public sector and, more specifically, public education represent a significant source of new revenue for both corporate and for-profit interests. Public school budgets have, until recently, been insulated from privatization. As noted earlier, however, that wall is rapidly being torn down through both deregulation of public schooling and charter reform. The amount of dollars potentially in play for redistribution from the public to the private sector is substantial.

Presently, over a half trillion dollars is spent annually on public education nationally. The potential economic gain associated with privatizing public education through charters is substantial. Importantly, such gain is not restricted to for-profit charter networks. For such networks, the profit motive is clear and transparent. Less visible however are the ways in which nonprofits, the fastest-growing sector of the charter movement, also generate profits, making for a range of private vendors catering to a range of needs in a reorganized marketplace. We will now turn our attention to the economic gains and profit-making associated with both for-profit and nonprofit charter schooling. Equally important, the strain between profit-making/economic gain and classroom instruction investment is also explored.

## THE SLIPPERY QUESTION OF PROFIT
## AND THE CONSOLIDATION OF POWER

The evidence regarding the relationship between economic gain and concentration of power within a small elite circle and the mobilization for charter reform is incontrovertible. However, the data are, at this point, largely anecdotal and fragmented. No single data set exists that systematically detects and tracks the levels and dynamics of profit-making across the charter sector. What we do know, however, is that charter institutions are both more vulnerable to corruption in less regulated and less accountable political environments and a new market center for profit making. More to the point, the thin charter promise to deliver innovative, ever-more-effective forms of instruction through its deregulated, relatively autonomous schools is undermined by the growing momentum to capitalize a growing share of public education. To the extent that profit-making shapes a school's goals, curricula, and hiring practices, the quality of classroom instruction is ever more likely to be shortchanged.

Often overlooked in the rush to charter reform is the principal dynamic of the marketplace, profit-making. The market is structured around economic incentive and gain, ideological belief is of secondary importance. Ideology helps to legitimate shifts in public policy, economic incentive drives it. The shift to deregulated, privatized forms of charter schooling is no exception. This section will illustrate through case example, the kinds of profit-making and economic benefit proliferating as a result of public education deregulation or charter schooling. As noted, it is not the intention of this discussion to offer a comprehensive understanding of the precise scope or dollar value of this capitalization of public education dollars. Instead, its intention is to pull back the veil of ideology to reveal the other face of charter reform: individual and corporate economic gain. Equally important, the discussion systematically explores the spectrum of mechanisms triggering economic gain through both for-profit and nonprofit charter schooling. In general, the opportunities to extract economic gain from charter reform are abundant and diverse.

As was noted earlier, charters are not organizationally homogenous. Rather, three primary options exist regarding the structure of charter schooling. These approaches include the following:

1.  Education management organizations, which are often for-profit supporters of charter chains
2.  Charter management organizations, or the nonprofit version of EMOs

3.  Stand-alone charters, which are typically set up by teachers, community groups, and school districts

For-profit charter networks, although outlawed in some states and sharing a checkered history, remain a significant player in charter schooling and reform. Although political and philanthropic decision-making has helped to shift the balance to nonprofit networks, the economic incentives and political support for profit-making charters remains robust in various parts of the country. The recent history of many of these networks, however, is most unsettling. For example, the Imagine Network, which is national in scope, was investigated in 2010 by Policy Matters Ohio. The report uncovers a web of profit-making ventures often hidden and of questionable legality that are spun from charter revenue and relationships. It is noted that Imagine and its real estate subsidiary company, Schoolhouse Finance, continue "using the kinds of complex real estate deals for which they were criticized in other states" (Van Lier, 2010). More specifically, Schoolhouse Finance has purchased, renovated, and leased buildings. This subsidiary sold five of the properties to "real estate investment trusts (REITs), then leased the properties back from the REITs and continued renting them to its schools, allowing opportunities for profit both at resale and as at it collects rent" (Van Lier, 2010). Importantly, the lease costs suggest that every school is paying a premium price for its physical facility that increases with each passing year, leaving less and less public money for classroom instruction. Equally important, the data regarding these transactions are not publicly available because Imagine is a privately held company. Therefore, we know little of the complex and often high rates of profit-making. Imagine is not an anomaly. To the contrary, profit-making is a principal goal of most management organizations across the country.

The clearest evidence of the nexus between economic gain and charter schooling is the substantial size of the for-profit sector of the movement. Approximately half of management organizations nationally are for-profit enterprises. The proliferation of for-profit EMOs has been especially evident in both the Midwest and South.

It is within this context that Alex Molnar notes

[The Edison Project's] original premise held that the company could profit by offering better results than existing public schools without additional resources. . . . The ink was barely dry on the Philadelphia agreement when Edison asked for $1,500 more per pupil. . . . The company ultimately settled for half that amount. Almost immediately thereafter, it began to lay off 211 employees and refused to take delivery on textbooks . . . pleading poverty despite an 11.8 million dollar contract. How else did Edison save money? By closing libraries and replacing them with [a] computerized test taking drill system devised by Edison called Benchmarks. Perhaps most disturbing was the misleading data released by Edison on its students' performance. In Michigan, Texas, Pennsylvania, Nevada, and Kansas, the performance of Edison's schools [was] described by officials as consistently underperforming in relationship to their public school counterparts. In Dallas; Clark County, Nevada; and Wichita, Kansas, a large number of Edison's charters made the list of failing or inadequate schools. (Molnar, 2005, p. 99)

The record of another large national for-profit vendor, White Hat, is equally distressing. Recently, 10 charter-governing boards in two states have questioned contracts between White Hat Management and its schools. The governing boards litigation states that White Hat's interest in "making a profit conflicts with the school's goal to educate" (Marshall, 2010, p. 2). The governing board further noted that these arrangements were "one sided" and described elements of the contract as "arbitrary" and not in the "best interest of the school" (Marshall, 2010, p. 2).

Educational Alternatives Inc. (EAI) is another nationally ambitious for-profit charter management company. In the mid-1990s, journalists began questioning the spending patterns, fiscal accountability practices, and testing results of EAI. In Minnesota and Baltimore, Maryland, EAI was exposed for spending more money than public schools, failing to deliver on its promises, and falsifying test results. In Hartford, Connecticut, a few years after its initial contract and promise to increase academic performance, EAI proposed to eliminate 300 teaching positions. Simultaneously, it proposed to charge the city $1.2 million "for first class air travel, two downtown condominiums and legal fees" (Molnar, 2005, p. 197). The *Hartford Courant* reported that the debate on EAI was tearing the "City's soul" (Molnar, 2005). By 1995, the City of Hartford had dramatically curtailed the role of EAI in managing its schools. In 1995, Baltimore officials reported they were canceling EAI's contract with the city.

The questionable practices of Dennis Bakke and his management company, Imagine, were also recently investigated in Arizona. Reporters discovered that his company has placed a charter school building in Sierra Vista on the market for $6.3 million, with 5 years left on the lease. The listing indicates that Imagine makes $456,968 per year from the tenant. The building presently is 100% occupied by students and faculty (Van Lier, 2010). Imagine has profited from its relationship to charter schooling in two ways. First, it was able to buy a building because of the revenue stream of its charter management fees and, in turn, that transaction accrued gains in equity. In addition, it profited from the annual leasing of the building to the school. Such profit-making produces substantial tradeoffs in the quality of instruction. The management and leasing fees paid to Imagine are substantial and derived from dollars otherwise allocated to classroom instruction. Herein lies the rub in the reallocation of public money from the classroom to profit-making ventures.

The twinning of profit maximization and underinvestment in classroom instruction/teacher support reflects a dynamic that is consistently reproduced in for-profit charter management companies. This should not be surprising: the failures of Edison, White Hat, EAI, and Imagine are not the exception but the rule. They are the consequence of incentives largely about maximization of profit and consequent underinvestment of resources in teaching and learning. This is accomplished by extracting profit from reduced costs of labor, programming, and facilities. As with other private sector companies, however, such practices do not extend to first tier managers who make substantial salaries and enjoy a range of perks. And recent exposure of corruption, fraud, waste, and other questionable practices has challenged our faith in the private sector as free from the presumed corruption and greed of bureaucracy.

In the last decade, however, the expansion of for-profit EMOs has slowed while the growth of nonprofit EMOs has accelerated. Indeed, foundation grants totaling almost $500 million were invested between 1999 and 2009 in this sector of charter reform, which includes some of the most notable networks, including Achievement First, KIPP, Aspire, Uncommon Schools, Green Dot, and Yes Prep. Over the last three years, the data indicate that nonprofit forms of charters are the most rapidly expanding sector of charter reform. Libby indicates, "The Edison debacle smeared the for-profit name [which was already opposed by most, but not all, of those in education circles] and further attempts have been only moderately successful. The business model seems too risky politically and there's not a lot of evidence it works" (Libby, 2010a).

Although the nonprofit sector is rapidly growing, the number of for-profit charter continues to represent about half of the total number of networks (Miron & Urshel, 2009). As Miron and Dingerson indicate, in an atmosphere of rapid expansion and likely overwhelmed authorizers providing oversight, conditions may be ripe for corruption (Miron & Dingerson, 2009). They further note that "a rapidly expanding sector might also attract inexperienced entrepreneurs . . . [who] may think it is an avenue for private gain. Private management companies play a role, too, because they are often used as vehicles to propagate charters." These private management organizations provide various forms of infrastructural support to both nonprofit and for-profit networks of charter schools (Miron & Dingerson, 2009, p. 30). Libby notes that only 12% of charters are run by management organizations, but they are concentrated in five states—California, Texas, Arizona, Illinois, and Ohio. Importantly, the CREDO Stanford data show that "four of the five states posted negative student achievement results while the fifth, California, showed no significant difference in student performance between charter schools and traditional public schools" (Miron & Dingerson, 2009, p. 30). In the poorly performing states, "a much higher proportion of charters are run by for-profit management organizations" (p. 30). Through the window of charter networks we begin to see the tangled vines of politics, money, and charter schooling. Consider the *New York Daily News* editorial from April 4th, 2010—in New York state for-profit charter schools are prohibited and only nonprofit options can be authorized. In this context, however, a number of internal stakeholders such as for-profit management companies and board-member politicians have profited from their relationship to nonprofit charter schools. This point was raised in a *Daily News* article, which indicated that "New York charter schools must not become playgrounds for cheap politicians. The warning signs are up: The lampreys who swim in the Legislature and City Council have begun to view charters as one more vehicle for plunder and patronage."

Charter schools are privately run public schools that operate under the auspices of one of three sanctioning agencies: the city's Department of Education, the state Board of Regents or the State University of New York. All must reject applications sponsored by elected officials and their kith and kin. This is the only way to prevent the appearance, if not the fact, of favoritism in awarding a charter or deciding whether to renew one in the case of a failing school.

To do otherwise will be to risk a scandal that undermines confidence in what has become one of the most effective school reforms in New York history. The muck is already rising. In Queens, state Sen. Majority Leader Malcolm Smith and Rep. Gregory Meeks got their mitts on two charter schools that have been swept up in a federal grand jury probe of the two officials' finances, which are, umm, complicated.

Meanwhile, the students have lousy quarters, and one of the schools provides a comparatively deficient education. The 300 kids who attend the Peninsula Preparatory Academy Charter School in Far Rockaway sit in trailers in a lot behind a chain-link fence, surrounded by piles of dirt, with no labs, gym, playground or cafeteria kitchen.

Founded by Smith, who was joined on the board by Meeks, Peninsula moved there after comfortably occupying space in Middle School 53. Why the shift? It could be because the site is owned by a developer called the Benjamin Companies.

Employees and affiliates gave almost $150,000 to Smith's campaigns. He funneled more than a half-million dollars to the firm, earmarked for preparing construction of a school building. There is as yet no visible evidence of this, although the company has used the school as a selling point for housing it hopes to build on a surrounding tract.

As if all this weren't bad enough, Peninsula is run by a for-profit company called Victory Schools, whose founder, Steven Klinsky, is a Smith donor. Plus, the kids are lagging. Peninsula received Cs on its last two school report cards.

Smith and Meeks have also been board members of the Merrick Academy Charter School. Housed in a converted bowling alley in Queens Village, the school has a leaky roof, no gym or playground and inadequate heat.

The school made three small political donations to Smith. An architect who—for free—worked on the bowling alley was at the same time working on a home Smith was renovating. He also later designed a home for Meeks. (*Daily News*, 2010)

In the Bronx, City Councilwoman Maria del Carmen Arroyo directed $1.5 million toward building a permanent facility for the South Bronx Charter School for International Culture and the Arts. "The school was headed by her nephew Richard Izquierdo Arroyo, who pleaded guilty last month to embezzling $115,000 from an unrelated taxpayer-funded nonprofit, partly to pay for trips and meals for himself, his aunt and his grandmother Assemblywoman Carmen Arroyo" (NYSUT, 2010c).

The corruption and greed found in both the for-profit and not-for-profit sectors and overreliance on management organizations raises serious questions about infrastructural and fiscal sustainability. Libby suggests the following:

The most damning part of the report focuses on the financial sustainability of CMO's [sic]. . . they didn't go with creating an infrastructure that could support stand alone charter or services that would support community driven grassroots charters . . . and CMO's didn't take into consideration the diseconomies of scale that result from a growing institution: the need for more employees as you expand into different grade levels; new employees to support opening schools; expansion into new markets and the need for quality control as the organization grows. . . . *None of the 10 CMO's visited by CRPE* [Center for Reinventing Public Education] *have reached their own definition of financial sustainability* [emphasis added]. (Libby, 2010b, p. 5)

The question of sustainability is entangled with the question of scale. The presumed benefit of these corporate networks is their capacity to "go to scale." Yet evidence suggests that "scale" often turns out to be financially costly, and educationally inefficient, with opportunities for corruption. It is within this context that many are raising questions about the long-term sustainability of these CMOs. When privately managed charters fail, who is responsible? Where do the children go? How does the public recoup our tax dollars? To whom are these schools accountable when they are open and, even more so, when they close? Is there a charter morning-after?

## PARTNERSHIP AND PROFIT IN THE GAME OF EDUCATIONAL PRIVATIZATION

The economic dynamics of nonprofit charters are not simply driven by internal or school/network-specific forces. To the contrary, nonprofit charters and their boards, as well as their management networks, are in an ongoing relationship with external stakeholders who profit from or gain fiscal benefits from privatization. It is within this context that we will now briefly meet a whole new set of actors, recently arrived fiscal newcomers to the field of public education. The service industries that have been profiting from nonprofit charter schooling include, but are not limited to, firms leasing space, constructing buildings, providing janitorial support, and assisting with off-site record keeping. The most lucrative of these industries involves both leasing and constructing space for charter schools.

More to the point, real estate interests stand to make potentially large profits. A particularly striking example of such profit-making is a venture-capital investment company, Entertainment Properties Trust (EPT), which entered this market in 2005. EPR has developed what it describes as triple net leases. EPR is the landlord, buying buildings in low-income communities, leasing them to charters, and "filling a need." The tenant pays for maintaining the buildings and running the classrooms. The tenant, according to journalist Daniel Wolff, "is in this instance the charter school operator Imagine, founded in 2004 serving 36,000 children from New York to Arizona" (Wolff, 2009). The result has been a first-rate investment because the tenant has been a dependable source of revenue through school taxes. Unfortunately, the cost of the lease accounts for half of the per-student revenue received by a number of the schools. Clearly, as one administrator remarked, "that is an enormous percentage of your budget to pay for classrooms" (p. 3). The benefit of stable classroom space provided by the leasing and venture capital firm has been offset by the educational cost of redirecting public money from the classroom to for-profit real estate entrepreneurs.

Potential profit-making for the real estate industry, however, is not limited to leasing arrangements. In New York City, for example, hundreds of millions of tax-levy dollars go to the construction of charter facilities. Clearly, this is an emergent and significant area of profit-making for a construction industry that has been wounded by the collapse of both the housing market and the curtailment of mortgage lending by the banking industry. Perhaps the most vivid example of this possible interplay of political power and economic investment is the allocation of $26 million to the PAVE charter school in Brooklyn, New York, to build a private facility for 350 children. It is within this context that *Daily News* reporter Juan Gonzalez wrote:

> Wealthy investors and major banks have been making windfall profits by using a little known federal tax break to finance new charter-school construction. The program is so lucrative that a lender who uses it can almost double his money in seven years.
>
> In Albany, which boasts the state's highest percentage of charter enrollments, a non-profit called the Brighter Choice foundation has employed The New Markets Tax Credit to arrange private financing for five of the city's nine charter schools.
>
> But many of those same schools are now straining to pay escalating rents, which are going toward the debt service that Brighter Choice incurred during construction. The result has been less money in per pupil state aid to pay operating costs.
>
> You would think that these financial problems would raise eyebrows among state regulators—or at least those charter school boards. But the powerful charter lobby has so far successfully battled to prevent independent audits of how its schools spend their state aid. And key officers of Albany's charter school boards are themselves board members, employees, or former employees of the Brighter Choice Foundation and its affiliates.
>
> If wealthy investors and banks can double their money simply by building charter schools, taxpayers deserve to know exactly who arranged these deals, who will benefit and what they will ultimately cost each school. (Gonzalez, 2010)

Public monies earmarked for charter construction will likely grow in the next decade. The expansion will be in large part driven by the rapidly expanded number of charters and the continuing scarcity of building space. The deep recession and its drag on the construction industry are not likely to abate in the near future. In turn, this economic slowing of new construction will draw public subsidies for a range of building projects to prop up this sector of the economy. Given the demand for and undersupply of charter buildings, public money is likely to flow in increasing volume to such projects. Within a stalled economy, these contracts will be highly prized. In turn, we can expect the banking and building industries to vigorously lobby for greater investment in charter construction and specific contracts. Importantly, such lobbying fueled by economic incentive creates yet another layer of advocacy for the expansion of charter schooling.

Another nonprofit, profit-making venture linking curriculum entrepreneurs and charter schooling was discovered in New York City. A new school proposed for Manhattan, the New York Flex Charter School, is being organized by a team of private investors in an education corporation, K–12, developing a hybrid learning model that employs individualized online learning and virtual instruction, along with actual instruction by classroom teachers (Zelon, 2010). The charter school is seen as a kind of laboratory to test and sell its technology in a new market, New York City. These curricula tools were a favorite of former New York City school chancellor Joel Klein, who believes hybrid learning offers a chance to shake up traditional education (Zelon, 2010). The company, founded in 1999 and traded on the New York Stock Exchange, is trumpeted through corporate PR as being the nation's premier provider of online curricula. Critical to this discussion, the involvement of K–12 in the charter school through both board membership and curricula commitment will test the state's new charter schools law, which forbids for-profit charter school management.

## CLAIMING MARKET SHARE:
## STRATEGIC ORGANIZING OF THE CHARTER CAMPAIGN

While individual charter schools might or might not serve well the children in their community, the charter school campaign's influence on national policy is ultimately a deception, fueled by a hybrid of benevolent, generous, and self-serving interests—a policy that benefits a few at the expense of many—at seemingly no cost, a market based political solution grafted onto growing inequality and an intensifying neglect of social crises in the poorest urban areas. Further, it is a no-accountability design, hollowing public schools as democratic institutions and practices (with accountability to parents and community) and a fragile/flawed infrastructure for equity.

In the charter campaign, we hear echoes of the subprim mortgages nightmare and the recurring corruption of for-profit, higher education proprietary institutions. All of these are iconic stories haunting communities of color as politically backed, market-branded "solutions" to long festering problems of the unequal distributions of private and public resources and structural racism within housing and education. Recently, in the housing market affordable loans were offered with little down for the mortgage but the terms rapidly ballooned, leaving many borrowers without their houses or original assets. This, in turn, produced new waves of homelessness and cascading desperation and despair. Simultaneously, the for-profit industry in higher education has produced spiraling debt and default as well as dead-end work opportunities for the very poor students of color who disproportionately attend such schools. Finally, charter schooling is expanded and presented as the answer to the public education crisis with little attention paid to evidence of academic outcome, fiscal accountability, and equal access. The nexus between economic gain—be it administrative salary or profit-making—and the proportion of public dollars that reach the classroom is largely ignored.

Our perspective is grounded in recent history and echoes of structural racism and privatization, which has taught us that growing *inequality* has been the persistent outcome of marketplace dynamics. Over the course of the past thirty years, U.S. citizens have witnessed a growing inequality of wealth and income. For example, the top 1% of Americans own 35% of the wealth (they owned 20.5% in 1979). Equally startling is that the top 5% own 62% of the wealth. Every study on inequality has traced this growing gap to ever-more-regressive tax codes and the dynamics of capital that in deregulated marketplaces concentrates wealth and income (Reich, 2010). These dynamics have intensified since the economic meltdown of 2008.

Turning away from the sores of cumulative crisis, charter reformers are either naïve or simply self-interested. Clearly, the transition from charter experiment to political movement, stimulating an insatiable appetite for replacing public schools with charters, marks the moment when the fundamental character and threat of this market reform has been placed in vivid relief.

To enact policies of market solutions to public problems requires political campaigns and power. The campaigns must offer policy solutions that provide a straightforward market-based political solution to public-education failure, hold schools singularly accountable for their difficulties, and conceal the historic underfunding and defunding of neighborhood schools. The campaigns developed by the charter movement have incorporated such messaging and themes into their political practice. The political agenda and broadest intention of the charter movement is to replace public schools with charters. The most compelling articulation of this strategic vision has been developed by Andy Smarick, a Bush domestic advisor in 2008, now consulting with the New Jersey Department of Education:

> Here, in short, is one roadmap for chartering's way forward: first, commit to drastically increasing the charter market share in a few select communities until it is the dominant system and the district is reduced to a secondary provider. The target should be 75%. Second, choose the targeted communities wisely. Each should begin with a solid charter base (at least 5% of market share), a policy environment that will enable growth (fair funding, non district authorizers, and no legislated caps), and a favorable political environment (friendly elected officials, editorial boards, a positive experience with charters to date, and unorganized opposition). This solution isn't an improved traditional district; it's an entirely different delivery system. . . . Charter advocates should strive to have every urban public school be a charter.
>
> Choose communities wisely and commit to increasing charter market share. For example, in NYS a concerted effort could be made to site in Albany or Buffalo a large percentage of the new charter schools allowed under the raised cap. Other potentially fertile areas include Denver, Detroit, Kansas City, Milwaukee, Minneapolis, New Orleans, Oakland, and DC.
>
> As chartering increases its market share in a city, the district will come under growing financial pressure. The district despite educating fewer and fewer students, will require a large administrative staff to process payroll and benefits and oversee special education programming, the districts per pupil costs will sky rocket.
>
> *At some point the district . . . will be financially unsustainable (and reduced) to a marginal player, the city's investors and stakeholders-taxpayers, foundations, business leaders, elected officials, and editorial boards are likely to demand a fundamental change. That is eventually when the financial crisis will become a political crisis.* It is within this context that the district could voluntarily begin the shift to an authorizer, developing a new relationship with its schools and reworking its administrative structure. . . . Or, believing the organization is unable to make the change, the district could gradually transfer its schools to an established authorizer. (www.schoolmatters.info, 2010, emphasis added)

How did this happen? How has this movement mobilized under our watch?

As was noted earlier, the charter movement was originally designed as an alternative within public education, a stimulus for innovation, eager to work with unions where possible, relying upon test scores to assess evidence of outcomes. In a very short period of time, however, the movement came to be fueled by campaigns and ads that circulate very damning information about public schools, attack teachers and unions, and are moving away from test scores as evidence of student performance and toward test scores as a vehicle for getting rid of bad teachers. In a short period of time, the movements' oppositional commitments have risen to the surface.

We analyze here five linked elements of the campaign:

1. Discrediting public education
2. Branding charters as educational innovation
3. Mobilizing the private sector—foundations and hedge funds (discussed earlier in this chapter)
4. Demonizing teachers and unions
5. Systematically ignoring all of the evidence of public sector innovation and success (discussed in the prior chapter)

## Discrediting Public Education While Branding Charters as Innovation

"Charter schools are replacing Catholic schools as the new second class system for the working class, upwardly mobile—creating enormous conflicts among families in the same community and same building" (Gonzalez, 2010).

In the aggregate, charters have sited their schools in poor communities of color. In large part, that choice can be attributed to these communities' profound need for effective schooling and frustration with the public system. Such decision-making, therefore, makes both policy sense and practical sense. Importantly, the poorest communities have enormous pent-up demand for new forms of education, long betrayed by the state and the private sector. New education products like charter schools, however, must be sold to parents/consumers if they are to channel that demand into an exit choice from public education. More specifically, the product has to be branded in ways that make it both immediately recognizable, on the one hand, and define it as more effective on the other. Like SUVs that are represented as the most rugged or coffee characterized as having the best taste and greatest caffeine kick, charter schools have to both identify and then create the magnetic field of allure for their targeted consumers.

The frustration of poor parents of color with public schooling in combination with the steady drumbeat that repetitiously names test scores and academic success as one and the same has caused parents to increasingly search for schools that offer the greatest promise of improving their child's testing performance and, in turn, life chances. And yet, the braiding of public sector critique and charter marketing is highly suspect. Why isn't there simply a campaign to advance charters within the public sector without the accompanying assault on all that is public? Consider the language in "Flooding the Zone," a brochure on charter strategy published by Democrats for Education Reform (DFER):

> Six mailings were sent to a universe of 15,000–35,000 families and 200,000 leaflets were placed under doors at every one of Harlem's public housing complexes. . . . Some mailings simply informed parents that they had a choice in where to send their children to school and urging them to make the most of it. Other mailings specifically advertised the four charter schools operated by SCN but kept to the same messaging. . . . One ad in the Harlem portion read, "Don't settle. You have the right to choose your child's school." (Democrats for Education Reform, 2008, p. 4)

Another ad announced, "Too many of our kids in Harlem can't read at grade level. What's the problem? The problem is our schools" (Democrats for Education Reform, 2008, p. 4). The implicit message was that charter schools outperform a failed public system and choice is the only answer to both parent and student despair.

In their own words, Democrats for Education Reform launched a campaign "messaging . . . the longstanding failure of education status quo" (Democrats for Education Reform, 2008, p. 1). They assumed that poor parents did not appreciate the value of "available" school options. They critiqued politicians who support public education. Perhaps more shameful, they encouraged 5,000 parents to show up for a lottery in which 4,400 would be losers. Indeed, one analysis estimates that the Harlem Success Charter Network alone spent $1.2 million recruiting applicants (Gonzalez, 2010). This is an astounding figure in an era of intensifying scarcity of public dollars for education. As well, this expenditure challenges the "social truth" that if you build it (charter exit options) parents will come with little or no prodding. Referring to this overt manipulation of parent presence and voice as democracy ultimately subverts and cheapens any larger democratic intention to transform public education on the basis of parent input and experience.

Two years later, in the spring of 2010, DFER launched another campaign to lift the cap for charter schools. In this instance the incentives of Race to the Top money sharply aligned with the advocacy objectives to more than double the number of charters in New York state. This effort vividly illustrates the careful alignment of powerful interest groups around a common agenda to rapidly expand charter education. How else does one explain, for example, more than 10 articles being published in the three major New York City newspapers on the advantages of charter education at precisely the moment when the question of lifting the cap was before the state legislature? The especially partisan and persuasive character of a number of the articles was heightened through a referencing of powerful figures, such as Bill Clinton, on the advantages of charter schooling.

This media blitz was, in part, intended to convince Sheldon Silver, the one state powerbroker resistant to a no-strings-attached policy of lifting or eliminating ceilings, to change his position. Silver advocated for a level playing field for charters and public schools, lifting the ceilings and equity in public allocations of resources in return for more rigorous forms of accountability and removing private interests from the governance of charter schools. Charter advocates have referred to Silver's proposal as a poison pill, but it is only a poison pill if advocates have in mind receiving public money to create institutions that are not accountable to public agencies or taxpayers.

## The Vilification of Teachers and Their Unions

With much encouragement from the federal government's Race to the Top initiative, the charter reform movement has explicitly linked the failure of public education to bureaucratic regulation, especially teachers and their unions. Critically, this political and public attack does not address either the empirical record of charter schooling in improving student achievement, equity, or graduation rates, or its churning of teachers. More to the point, in this campaign the straw man of public school failure is elevated while the performance of charter schools is closeted. The problem, according to charter advocates and their allies, is that these unions have protected incompetent classroom instructors, supported a tenure system that guarantees lifetime employment to teachers not producing results in the classroom, resisted new forms of measurable accountability, and lobbied legislators with substantial resources to protect their interests, which, more often than not, are in conflict with the needs of the most learning-challenged students in urban areas.

In turn, we would challenge the assumptions of charter-movement reformers and some of their right-wing allies that teachers and their unions are the source of public education breakdown in the poorest neighborhoods. Granted, teacher unions have predictably resisted measures that would weaken job security for their members. And at times, that resistance has protected teachers who have not performed adequately in the classroom. That said, in general, for years teachers in public schools have struggled with conditions that are at best difficult and at worst impossible. Too often, the best efforts of public school teachers are washed away by the decay of the physical plant, overcrowded classrooms, an increasing sense of professional isolation, and overwhelmed administrators who cannot find the time to provide necessary supports. For these and other reasons, the public schools churn their cohort of teachers at an alarming rate, which, in turn, has a substantial impact on academic performance. The public flaying of teachers for the failure of public education simultaneous with the rapidly accelerating turnover of staff because of working conditions is politically pivotal for charter reform. It is far easier and cheaper to sell teachers as the villains in the melodrama of public school failure than to dramatically rethink the kinds and levels of investment we are making in the poorest communities of color and the supports we are (not) offering educators in these communities.

The political campaign to vilify teachers and pave the way for charter reform also has an economic objective. The reduction of teachers' wages has been, at least, part of the intention and impact of charter schooling. Wages are pegged to longer school years and days. Stipulations regarding job protection or security are rapidly stripped away, as charters are largely union free environments. Health- and pension-benefit packages are also substantially less for charter school teachers than for unionized teachers. Workers' capacity to organize or unionize around these issues is also restricted. So, let us make no mistake, part of the intention of the public-sector decision makers and their allies is to reduce the power of the one institution that can contest the exercise of unilateral managerial power—unions. As the unchallenged power of corporate elites, public-sector managers, and their political allies sets both the direction and frame of the discourse regarding public education policy, increasingly absent from these discussions are the voices of professionals and communities immersed in the day-to-day work of creating a public education.

As was noted earlier there are moments when the interests of public union members and the interests of those they serve may be in conflict. Too often in the recent past, teacher unions have not found ways to align their interest with those of parents and students. Concerns of structural racism have often been elided by labor. Teacher salaries and job security were often pitted against many poor communities, often compelling need for other forms of investment such as lower student-to-instructional staff ratios; economic incentives for effective, seasoned instructors to remain in resource-starved neighborhoods; and the removal of ineffective teachers from the classroom. The lack of attention to these differences and the need to organize more collaborative relationships has produced significant divisions between parents and teachers as well as their unions. We believe we are witnessing some change in this landscape that links issues of educators' rights with questions of community participation and structural racism (Fabricant, 2010). It is within this context that a number of progressive caucuses running on platforms of labor-community partnership have prevailed within education-union elections, most particularly for instance in Chicago. In New York City radical caucuses of educators, such as NYCORE (New York Coalition of Radical Educators) and GEMS (Grassroots Education Movement), are crafting significant coalitions between educators, youth, and community. Importantly, at the level of policy, community organizing, and school reform, these new social movements are only working at the edges of traditional union concerns and strategies for educational justice. The integration of community social movement and union political work on matters of public education therefore remains an especially critical and daunting challenge.

## The Charter Campaign's Erasure of Public-Sector Innovation

Needless to say, the meteoric ascent of charter schooling and the simultaneous, expansive sightings of "exemplars" have made it increasingly difficult for innovative public schools to grab media attention. Indeed, some have been punished for their innovation, others pressured to conform and standardize—particularly along the lines of high-stakes testing—and many denied the very "freedoms" to innovate that the charters have been provided. Other times the stories of public school success have just been buried. Consider, for instance, Jay Mathews's article in the July 2010 *Washington Post*, "Class Struggle," in which he admits:

> I have to question my own judgment and fair mindedness when I ignore—for three years!—a report that raises important questions about the way we have been using test scores to rate schools.
>
> I have always been open to better ways of assessing how our children are taught. But I usually say standardized tests are the best available tool at the moment. So I am embarrassed that it took me so long to read "Keeping Accountability Systems Accountable" by Martha Foote, published in the Phi Delta Kappan education journal in January 2007.
>
> I am indebted to the Monty Neill, executive director of Fairtest: the National Center for Fair and Open Testing, for pointing me toward the article and its author. Foote is director of research for the New York Performance Standards Consortium, which she describes in her article as "a coalition of 28 small, diverse public high schools across New York State that exemplify education reform based on strong commitment to school-as-community, to ongoing professional development, and to innovative curricula and teaching strategies." That sounds good to me, but it gets better.
>
> Recognizing that their students learn best when actively engaged, consortium schools typically use inquiry-based methods of learning with classrooms steeped in discussion, project-based assignments, and student choice. Con-

sortium schools are also committed to using complex, performance-based assessments to gauge student learning, with four specific performance tasks required of all students for graduation.

## COLLATERAL DAMAGE: THE LOSS OF ACCOUNTABILITY

The complex individual motivations for charter reform are linked to a political economy that has its own dynamics. And all too often we witness that the public sector of education is where the collateral damage can be found. As Governor Christie of New Jersey cuts $1.3 billion of state monies from public education, he shows up on *Oprah* celebrating the infusion of $100,000,000 from Facebook, private monies that are contingent on the whim of an individual and not, of course, sustainable. At the same time, a number of foundations have invested $65 million in the Washington, DC, school system to promote merit pay.

Across a country, we are witnessing swelling budget deficits. The aggregated budget deficit for states across the country is expected to grow from $111 billion in 2009 to $180 billion in 2011 (American Federation of Teachers, 2009, p. i). In turn, every state is looking to private foundations and patrons to make up some part of that difference. And yet interestingly, some features of public education—for instance, the expensive and expansive testing regime—remain untouched by budgetary concerns. This same testing regime is of course the "scientific" engine behind school report cards, school closings, charter openings, and more of the punish-and-humiliate ridicule we call "accountability."

Critically, charter reform does not exist in a vacuum but rather is a part of the larger decline in public spending, growing inequality in wealth and income, and a marketplace that is always searching for new engines for profit-making. In turn, these dynamics contribute to the formation of politics of public scarcity of resources and propose policy solutions that are driven by the market solutions of choice, competition, and autonomy—but ironically no accountability. This political solution, however, too often both conceals and denies the underlying economic choices and assumptions driving political solutions.

The newest concern of charters to increase "market share," coordinated through shared CMOs or authorizing mechanisms, presents a number of threats to democratic accountability. As charters are governed by boards or management organizations that have a national or regional structure, they radically restructure public education by severing school from neighborhood and forging unclear relationships of accountability to local as well as state government. In general, this change in auspices of public education threatens to undermine essential elements of democracy as well as critical citizenship.

The growth of CMOs also raises questions about sustainability, the diseconomies of scale, and, of course, the deep question of equity and accountability. According to the market logic of charter reform parents are consumers, putting pressure on the system, as state responsibility for all children grows more and more intangible. Questions of public accountability accumulate and evaporate as state responsibility recedes:

- Who, for instance, worries about the children whose parents don't/can't get them into a charter, on a waiting list, or well placed?
- Who is responsible for tracking, educating, picking up the children who fall out of the "market"?
- Who educates the children asked to leave their charters?
- Where is the large public responsibility for equity in finances, opportunities, and outcomes?
- Who is responsible for overseeing processes that facilitate racial integration and shared democratic commitments?
- To whom do critical accountability functions of the public education system fall?
- Where do we grow engaged, inquiring, responsible citizens and thoughtful writers and critics in our multiracial democracy, not just competitive consumers competing for scarce opportunities in an unregulated marketplace?

## REFLECTIONS ON POLITICS, ECONOMICS, AND IDEOLOGY

The charter movement is increasingly focused on radical revamping of public education, injected with fiscal and legislative incentives from the Obama administration when it linked eligibility for Race to the Top funding to an expansion of charter schooling during a moment of fiscal and economic crisis. The political pressure exerted on state legislatures by local media and business interests to both seek federal money and accept whatever strings are attached has intensified.

The maximal amount of revenue available through Race to the Top, however, will not come close to filling state education budget gaps reported by the *Washington Post, New York Times,* and *Los Angeles Times.* Winners may see an additional $75 million to $100 million for new initiatives. In contrast, however, New York state has a projected education budget gap of $1.3 billion. Race to the Top occurs in a context in which the larger system of public education is retrenching teachers, watching class ratios soar, witnessing the physical decay of facilities without the ability to slow it, proliferating outdated equipment, and providing less and less support in and outside the classroom to instructors. These trends occur within the crisis of the larger economy, which has produced dramatically less tax revenue.

As the smoke of charter reform begins to clear, its impact becomes ever more apparent. The rationing of charter education has resulted in an increasing clamor for exit, an intensifying allure of all things private, and the migration of public resources out of neighborhood schools in the poorest areas. This intensifying disinvestment is accompanied by ever more symbolic forms of public education reform that substitute modest investments in a small number of communities and schools for needed levels of targeted investment. Clearly, the conditions necessary to reinvent learning and instruction conditions for a majority of poor students of color cannot be achieved within this intellectually arid and fiscally degraded reform box.

The bottom line is that if we are serious about education reform, it will require that the 95% of students not affected by charter schooling be paid equal attention. Levels of public resources must be directed to schools commensurate with their difficulty. These resources need to be channeled to education programming and practice on the basis of their empirical record of effectiveness. Ever wider circles of parent participation need to be systematically fostered to produce the kinds of community-school partnerships necessary to raise the academic achievement of neighborhoods of students.

Ultimately, charter policy hides a profound failure of political will—more specifically, a failure of business, legislative, and media leadership to support the kinds of budgets, taxation, and targeted investment necessary to revive public education as a key element of social and economic development and racial justice in the poorest communities. Politicians looking for safety find political cover through popular reform requiring no new taxes while promising improved academic performance. Interlocking interests are simply unwilling to make the difficult policy choices and investments necessary to improve the educational and community life in the poorest urban neighborhoods and instead are drawn to the quick-fix solution and economic gains of anemic reforms such as charter schooling.

# CHAPTER 5

# "Crisis": A Moment for Dispossession and Profit

In November of 1910, W. E. B. Du Bois published the first issue of *The Crisis: A Record of the Darker Races*. The title of the NAACP magazine was drawn from a poem by James Russell Lowell. Published in 1844, "The Present Crisis" narrates the "low foreboding cry of those Crises" that "jut through Oblivion's seas."

Both Lowell and Du Bois insisted that a record be kept of the ongoing crisis of "the darker races." Du Bois launched *The Crisis* with that bold political intent:

> The object of this publication is to set forth those facts and arguments which show the danger of race prejudice, particularly as manifested today toward colored people. It takes its name from the fact that the editors believe that this is a critical time in the history of the advancement of men. Finally, its editorial page will stand for the rights of men, irrespective of color or race, for the highest ideals of American democracy, and for reasonable but earnest and persistent attempts to gain these rights and realize these ideals. (Du Bois, 1910)

We begin our discussion of "crisis" in the historic and contemporary miseducation of children of color and poverty, grounded in Du Bois's recognition that crisis, for poor people and people of color in the United States, has been woven deeply into the bloody fabric of our nation's history (Woodson, 2010). Public schools have been institutions in which crisis has festered and been washed over by oblivion's sea, where cries could hardly be heard, if muffled. Structured in ways that reproduce class and racial stratifications (Anyon, 1997; Bell, 1993; Bowles & Gintis, 1977; Delpit, 2006; Fine, 1991; Kozol, 1972; Woodson, 2010), public schools have also, at times, been mobilized by the vibrant energy of dedicated communities, progressive educators, and engaged youth to contest social injustice and advocate for social transformation (e.g., Anand, Fine, Perkins, & Surrey, 2002; Ayers & Tanner, 2010; Cook & Tashlik, 2005; Karp, 2006, 2010; Lipman, 2011; Meier, 2002; Moses & Cobb, 2002; Payne & Strickland, 2008; Walker, 1996). And yet the systemic miseducation of children of color stains our national history (Woodson, 2010). The structural and historic educational cri(s)es have been routinely ignored until they are not. Lowell implores us to take note of when the "stern winnowers" decide to listen to the "low foreboding cry" and "save" them. With increasing frequency, saving is only considered in direct relationship to profit. Today we hear the calls of "crisis," but Du Bois asks us to be suspect.

The charter movement was birthed in the midst of crisis. While our earlier writings acknowledge the deep and sustained inequities that have always characterized the struggle in poor communities for quality education, our intent in this chapter is to track critically how the crises of public education—real and ideological—have been produced by disinvestment and then "discovered" and exploited by voucher advocates and charter entrepreneurs, thereafter paving a path for the charter movement to roll into, and over, poor communities-of-color (Fabricant, 2010; Fine, 1991).

There is, then, a doubled crisis at the heart of this chapter. The structurally induced crisis in education recognizes the deep historic neglect and miseducation of poor, immigrant children and poor children-of-color, a long-festering enactment of internal colonialism. The ideological crisis, however, references those moments in history when corporations and the media have declared "crisis" and then marketed their products at the expense of poor communities of color. The dynamic structural and ideological crisis of education is vividly illustrated through charter reform. Corporations, philanthropists, and government have joined together to promote charters as an answer to the public education crisis in very poor communities, at the very moment that they advocate reduced funding for public education and other public services in low-income communities.

Draw a line from W. E. B. Du Bois, who chronicles the relentless, ongoing struggle in the Black community for quality education, to Naomi Klein's (2007) writing in *The Shock Doctrine: Disaster Capitalism*, in which she argues that immediately after neoliberal or imperial intervention, crises are often declared—in Iraq, Afghanistan, or New Orleans—and public assets as well as functions are systematically transferred from government to private, corporate interests. By linking Du Bois and Klein we make visible an old ideology of an exalted market that assures structural inequality and, in turn, concentrates specific forms of economic and political gain.

## IN A LANDSCAPE OF INEQUALITY: WHOSE CRISIS IS IT ANYWAY?

[S]ome African Americans are supportive of school choice because
they have little confidence in the quality of the schools their children
attend. They may not necessarily embrace a conservative perspective
on schooling and society. The traditional ideological spectrum in which
liberal is to the left and conservative is to the right just does not apply
to these parents and their experiences with education. These low
income African American families merely wanted what was best for their
children. (Morris, 2009, p. 156)

We have no doubt and substantial evidence that parents in many communities, largely African American, Latino, and immigrant, are deeply
distressed by the absence of quality education. We are equally convinced,
however, that the charter movement is now riding on the waves of the
deep despair and desires of low-income families seizing the tactical opportunity to privatize the public assets of mature welfare-state systems.
Because the decay of public services is particularly acute in the poorest
communities of color, they emerge as a critical front line in the war to
reengineer or privatize services.

What has preceded and followed privatization are decades of neglect
of public schools, health care, and social services in very poor communities. The very policies that ensure quality education and other human
rights for some youth fundamentally undermine these opportunities and
rights for others. For instance, a newly renovated selective high school,
replacing or co-located with a failing school will undoubtedly serve some
at the expense of those who have historically been underserved in the
same building. These circuits of dispossession and privilege widen inequality gaps and erode our commitment to democracy as an engine for
equity (Fine & Ruglis, 2008).

A number of scholars have noted that the fabric of society frays when
we invest unequally or disinvest in public education. Before we consider
how charters contribute to these inequality gaps, let us consider the most
recent evidence that inequality affects us all.

British epidemiologists Richard Wilkinson and Kate Pickett (2009)
have argued in *The Spirit Level: Why Greater Equality Makes Societies Strong*
that severely unequal societies produce high rates of "social pain": adverse outcomes including school dropout/pushout, teen pregnancy, mental health problems, lack of social trust, high mortality rates, violence and
crime, and low social participation (2009). Their volume challenges the
belief that the extent of poverty in a community predicts negative out-

comes. They assert instead that the size of the inequality gap defines the material and psychological contours of the chasm between the wealthiest and the most impoverished, enabling various forms of social suffering to saturate a community. These forms of suffering that can, over time, be misread as natural, either biological or cultural, are manifested through rates of incarceration, drug addiction, child abuse, suicide, infant mortality, literacy, and school dropout rates. Societies and communities with large gaps build gated communities for some and barbed-wire communities for others. As you might guess, the income inequality gap of the United States ranks highest internationally.

Political theorist David Harvey frames these dynamics as accumulation by dispossession: "dispossessing somebody of their assets or their rights . . . we're talking about the taking away of universal rights and the privatization of them so it [becomes] your particular responsibility rather than the responsibility of the State" (Harvey, 2004, p. 2). Layered on a landscape of inequality, educational dispossession is today animated by a series of federal and state policies that widen opportunity, and therefore, achievement gaps by race/ethnicity and social class. Drawing on Harvey's analysis of dispossession, Fine and Ruglis (2008) have documented how circuits of dispossession and privilege redistribute and redesign communities and young lives (2008), moving educational resources and dreams across zip codes. We rely upon a language of circuits so that we may track the blue dye of disinvestment and privatization traversing through and beyond public education, provoking structural-, institutional-, community-, and individual-level changes along the contours of racial/class fault lines.

In this chapter we look at how three cities, New Orleans, Chicago, and New York City, have authorized a quiet, subterranean stream of public education policies featuring charter schooling that are redistributing academic opportunities and outcomes.

There is nothing natural about these cumulative practices of dispossession—even if provoked by a flood. Consider the iconic charter city of crisis, New Orleans.

## AFTER THE FLOODS: CHARTER GROWTH IN NEW ORLEANS

I think the best thing that happened to the education system in New Orleans was Hurricane Katrina. That education system was a disaster, and it took Hurricane Katrina to wake up the community to say that "we have to do better." (Arne Duncan as quoted by Nick Anderson, Washington Post, 2010)

In a compelling volume entitled *Dismantling a Community,* the Center for Community Change (CCC) traces the post-Katrina educational transformation in New Orleans, chronicled by a collective of youth, journalists, artists, and educators mobilized in a project called Students at the Center (2008). Some parts of the story are well known:

> In late August 2005, Hurricane Katrina slammed into the Gulf coast. Among its many casualties, the storm shattered the New Orleans' public school system. Over half of the city's school buildings were destroyed. Tens of thousands of students and teachers fled across the country to find shelter, jobs, and an education. . . . But Katrina was just the beginning of a much more fundamental "end" to the New Orleans Public Schools. In the immediate chaos after the storm, many both in and outside New Orleans—people who were not searching for relatives, who had dry shoes, and a place to lay their heads—seized on the disaster as an "opportunity." . . . Over . . . twelve months, buoyed by the support of the federal government, a network of conservative and anti-government activists have moved with singular intensity to patch together a new vision for K–12 education that they hope will become a national model. It is a vision that disdains the public sector and those who work within it. It is a vision based on competition and economic markets. It is a vision of private hands spending public funds. (Center for Community Change, 2008, p. 1)

Some parts of the story of Katrina are less well known. Twelve days after the storm hit, the Education Industry Association, a group of corporations, textbook publishers, and educational entrepreneurs, seized the crisis and sent out the following letter to members: "Defining moments in history are often recognized with aid of hindsight. . . . The change is to see these moments in real time and to act decisively. Katrina, and her swath of destruction, can be one of these defining moments in the history of the education industry" (Center for Community Change, 2008, p. 2).

New Orleans emerged as a "green field" for educational transformation—privatization (Center for Community Change, 2008, p. 3). By October 2005, the Orleans Parish School Board voted 4–1 to transform all schools in the Algiers community into charters (13 schools in all). While the schools in the community were instructed to follow open-admission norms of public education, as charter schools, both the size and composition of the student body was determined by charter management. Equally important, the Parish decided to waive the requirement that charter conversion be approved by a school faculty. Within a month, an African American reverend filed suit against the new charter district, citing the need for community consultation. Judge Nadine Ramsey moved to stop the charter district development:

It is in this time of crisis, when the citizens of Orleans Parish are concerned about the very future of their communities, that the role of public input is crucial. The people of New Orleans are entitled to participate in the process that will potentially change the landscape of their public educational system. (Center for Community Change, 2008, p. 16)

We see the shift from community participation and ownership of schools to a more corporate, remote management.

Following Judge Ramsey's decision, the Orleans Parish board met and moved to have a public discussion on the conversion to charter schools. They then quickly revoted to establish the Algiers Charter School District, comprising the 13 schools originally identified on the west bank. The board also issued charters to seven east-bank schools, authorizing an expansion of the Lusher Middle and High School onto two charter campuses. Importantly, these charter schools occupied the land of the former Fortier High School. Fortier was a predominantly black, low-performing high school with close to 900 students prior to the storm. In the new Lusher configuration, the high school is highly selective with first priority granted to the children of professional staff at Tulane, Loyola, Dillard, and Xavier universities. We learn from the CCC report that:

When registration at Lusher begins, the school reaches capacity so quickly that even some former Lusher Elementary students are denied access to the middle school. In the months after the takeover of Fortier, Tulane University helps raise over 1.5 million dollars in private and public funds to renovate the Fortier Building. (Center for Community Change, 2008, 16)

By January 2006, 17 schools were opened in New Orleans: 3 public schools, 3 charters authorized by the Recovery School District (the legal body responsible for the public schools that performed at or below state average), 5 charters operated by Algiers Charter School District, and 6 charters run by other organizations. Another lawsuit was filed for the students turned away from their schools in neighborhoods of origin. In February, the Orleans Parish School Board decided to fire 7,500 teachers and school staff. Subsequent to that decision, new schools opened and established their own selective admissions criteria: 4 public schools, 7 charters run by Recovery School District, 6 run by Algiers Charter School District, and 8 independent charters. The board voted that each charter must admit a minimum of 10% students with disabilities, although all agreed there was little capacity for oversight.

On June 12, 2006, then Secretary of Education Margaret Spellings granted $24 million to Louisiana for the purpose of further expanding the number of charter schools as a part of the recovery. On June 14, the Recovery School District declared that it would postpone the creation of any RSD schools for 2006–2007, making clear that they had not hired a single teacher for its schools. By July 27, the Algiers Charter School Association announced plans to open 8 schools in the fall, with $12 million in its reserve fund. Jeanne Allen at the Center for Education Reform explains, "New Orleans is such a great example of what you can do if you start over" (Center for Community Change, 2008, p. 32).

Researchers from the Institute on Race and Poverty documenting the New Orleans transformation have found that charter schools "skim the most motivated" students through selective admissions, disciplinary measures, expulsion practices, transportation policies, location decisions, and marketing as well as recruitment efforts (Institute on Race and Poverty, 2010). They conclude:

> The new, post Katrina public school system in New Orleans is becoming more and more reliant on charter schools. The sector grew rapidly as a result of the coordinated efforts of a number of charter school proponents, in response to strong financial incentives (from the federal government and the philanthropic community) and not necessarily because of the superior educational performance of charters. . . . As charter schools begin replacing traditional public schools through school conversions, parents, students and teachers may be forced to choose a charter school because of the lack of high quality traditional schools. . . . When charter schools become the only option, rather than being one among many, choice options are narrowed for students. (Institute on Race and Poverty, 2010, p. 14)

Researchers found that *students of color* were particularly hurt by the racial and economic segregation that now characterizes New Orleans' schools, because they "largely attend non-White segregated schools with high concentrations of poverty while White segregated schools tend to have low rates of poverty" (Institute on Race and Poverty, 2010, p. 12).

In addition, they argue that "the increasingly charterized public school system has seriously undermined quality of opportunity among public school students" (p. 5). Further, they voice concern that "the continuing expansion of the charter sector is jeopardizing the very existence of the traditional public sector in the city. This type of predatory expansion runs counter to the promise of expanding school choice" (p. 5). And finally, they acknowledge that even advocates of charters recognize that the system is "saturated" (p. 5).

In New Orleans, charters are being offered up as the "silver lining" to the long-standing crisis of educational failure. Although the floods created the occasion, the disaster of public education had long accumulated from a history of systemic, racialized abuse and neglect. When the levees broke, a crisis for some became an opportunity for others—those "stern winnowers" Lowell so worried about.

New Orleans is a cautionary tale of educational reform. No one would argue that pre-Katrina schools were effective. To the contrary, it has been widely recognized that New Orleans public schools have long been held hostage to political favoritism and corruption. And yet, our concern has not been in the redevelopment of the school district, not even in the growth of the charter sector, but in the simultaneous disinvestment in public education, the extremely segregated nature of the New Orleans system, the loss of parent-community engagement with local schools, and the diminished access of neighborhood children to their local schools. More to the point, we witness an accelerated dispossession of communities and individuals by a radically deregulated and privatized education system. Deeply eroded is a trace of a public sphere organized through democratic deliberation and public institutions designed to cultivate the collective good. Instead, people in New Orleans, Katrina refugees in Texas who cannot return, and the rest of us bear witness to cumulative evidence of a state committed, by deed and intent, to the dispossession of many students and parents throughout the restructured system and to the cultivation of various form of profit. As the prior chapter underscored, charter profiteering in New Orleans and elsewhere comes in many forms—construction contracts, dividends to owners, profits for management companies, and outsourcing to infrastructural support companies—and is unrelentingly and dynamically associated with the deregulation of public education. Declaration of "crisis" has become the single most important source of legitimacy for deregulating education. In turn, this has led to further dispossessing and disorganizing communities in their relationship to local schooling as well as privatizing heretofore public assets.

The language and experience of "crisis" have a powerful reverberation in New Orleans. Extreme vulnerability in the wake of the physical catastrophe of Katrina made it especially ripe for the remaking of its school system. In Chicago, a mix of educational struggles and an aspiration for urban renaissance were the flames that bought charter reform to a boil.

## BUILDING AN EDUCATION RENAISSANCE: CHICAGO AND CHARTER EDUCATION

The Chicago story of educational dispossession links to the city's plan for Renaissance 2010, which Pauline Lipman and Davis Hursch (2007) describe as part of a larger project to raze low income African American communities, with the goal of gentrifying areas with new condominiums, luxury apartments, and retail services. Renaissance 2010 reveals the increasing ability of corporations to reshape both the city and the schools in their own interests. (p. 161)

Chicago's testing and accountability system set the stage for a series of school closings as well as charter and contract school openings:

> What the accountability regime did accomplish, intentionally or not, was a system of ranking school failure that established a necessary condition to identify schools to be closed. . . . Renaissance 2010 provides neither more funding for schools nor support for teachers but rather aims to improve schools by restructuring them as private-public ventures and by introducing markets and competition, therefore, ostensibly improving efficiency. (Lipman & Hursch, 2007, p. 166)

Under the umbrella of Renaissance 2010, Chicago Public Schools (CPS) closed scores of schools. The CPS website announces:

### Office of New Schools

The Office of New Schools (ONS) in the Chicago Public Schools is committed to creating new and innovative schools that will provide high quality educational options to serve the diverse needs of Chicago's public school students. These schools include "new starts" and "turnaround" schools which seek to transform struggling schools into quality educational options for Chicago students. ONS manages a portfolio of 86 schools that consist of all charter and contract schools developed through Renaissance 2010 and all charter schools created before Renaissance 2010.

### Renaissance 2010 Background and History

In 1997, the Illinois General Assembly approved 45 charter schools for the state of Illinois, including 15 for Chicago. In 2003, 15 additional charters were approved for Chicago. These innovative schools produced gains in student achievement, increased demand, and strong parent satisfaction. This set the stage for Renaissance 2010, an initiative designed to create more high quality educational options across Chicago.

In June 2004, Mayor Richard Daley launched Renaissance 2010, a bold initiative whose goal was to increase the number of high-quality educational options in communities across Chicago by 2010.

Despite the popularity of school closings as a reform *de jure,* there has been very little empirical analysis of its impact. An exceptional piece of research was undertaken in 2009 by the Consortium on Chicago School Reform to document the academic and social consequences of school closings on urban elementary school students in Chicago (de la Torre & Gwynne, 2009).

Tracking 5,445 K–8 students who had attended 44 of the Chicago Public Schools closed for poor academic performance or underutilization between 2001 and 2006, Consortium researchers found that most displaced students were transferred to equally weak schools—public, charters, and for-profit contract schools. One year after closing, no significant improvements in math or reading scores could be determined for the displaced students. In fact, the greatest loss in mathematics and reading achievement occurred during the chaotic year prior to the school closing, when plans were just announced and when the schools filled with the angst of institutional death and displacement.

The achievement levels (as measured by test scores) of a small group of displaced students did, however, improve. Students who transferred to schools with high academic strength and high levels of teacher trust and efficacy showed marked improvements in math and reading. However, only 6% of students transferred into such schools. A full 42% of students transferred into schools with low levels of trust or efficacy. Overall, then, in terms of academic improvement, these researchers "found few effects, either positive or negative of school closings on the achievement of displaced students" (de la Torre & Gwynne, 2009).

Two disturbing findings, however, deserve mention. First, many of the closed neighborhood schools were later reopened as charters but not accessible to neighborhood students. Second, students from closing schools were significantly less likely to participate in Summer Bridge programs and had higher transfer rates across schools, from their first receiving school, than their Chicago Public School peers.

The interaction of high-stakes testing, declaration of school failure, school closings, charter expansion, and displacement reflects a straightforward enactment of policy initiatives intended to transport Hayek's marketplace supposition regarding the need to destroy prior institutional arrangements to create more effective and efficient arrangements to public education. The crisis of school failure as measured by standardized testing is the legitimating trigger for the rapid implementation of deregulation and displacement policies. The Renaissance of Chicago is being hosted in "an increasingly dual city" where as a matter of policy, the poorest students of color are increasingly likely to experience the dislocation and dispossession of replacing traditional neighborhood schools with charters.

Chicago has enjoyed a rich resistance movement—"the schools that are being closed . . . are almost entirely in African American communities experiencing gentrification" (Lipman & Hursch, 2007, p.170). The June 2010 election of new union leadership—in CORE (Caucus of Rank and File Education), a coalition of social justice educators—signals educators' commitment to challenging mayoral control. As Karen Lewis, CORE president, explains, "The union . . . is now unified . . . poised to reclaim power and what we love: teaching and learning in publicly funded public schools" (Lewis, 2010). Lewis vowed to fight expansion of charter schools and standardized tests, two parts of what she called the growing influence of corporations and profit in public schools situated within communities experiencing rapid gentrification over the last decade and a half. "We want to put business in its place and out of our schools," she said We turn now to New York City, the poster child for placing business at the heart of public education.

## DECLARING "CRISIS": SCHOOL CLOSINGS AND CHARTER OPENINGS IN NEW YORK CITY

In New York City, the mayor and chancellor have been closing failing schools with the justification of testing data, presumably to protect low-income communities from "bad education" (Otterman, 2010). While the academic track record of many of these schools has been admittedly dismal, responsibility for these outcomes lay largely with the historic disinvestment in urban low-income communities—intensifying but long-standing inequity of investment on the basis of race and class and the searing consequences of this fiscal abandonment. The political economy of public sector failure is wholly ignored when schools are declared failing and threatened with closure. Further, parents, guardians, community members, educators, and youth are systematically excluded from decisions to close schools and plans to redesign their replacements. The cover story about saving communities from educational crisis grows a bit suspect when the very communities presumably being saved are kept out of the process—and their children are often denied admission to the replacement schools.

Resistance, in New York as in Chicago, has been substantial. On January 27, 2010, at 3:30 a.m., the New York City Mayor's Panel for Educational Policy voted to close 19 schools for poor performance. This decision occurred after an auditorium of thousands of parents, educators, and youth testified for close to 9 hours, protesting the school closings. Parents complained there had been no community consultation and educators insisted there had been no educator consultation. Advocates for Children released a report documenting that the schools slated for closing were serving disproportionately homeless youth: the number of New York City students who were classified as homeless rose by

21% citywide from 2007–2008 to 2008–2009 but by, on average, 580%, on average, at the schools slated to be closed. Educators noted that the schools designated for closure had been assigned disproportionately high numbers of youth with special needs, without the appropriate supports (Gonzalez, 2010, p. A2).

Parents, community members, educators, and youth were, by many accounts, stunning in their resistance—armed with sock puppets to mock the mayoral appointees on the panel. And yet as anticipated, the Wednesday after, as schools filled with frustration, anger, defeat, and disappointment at democracy denied, Mayor Bloomberg told the press, "Last night we listened very carefully, and nobody made a good convincing case why we should let any student go one more day than we absolutely have to with a bad education" (Otterman, 2010).

As noted earlier, when schools are closed they are rarely reopened for the same group of children. Local children typically lose a school, while a local resource, public institution, and (potential or actual) site of community engagement disappears from communities. Local democratic processes for determining which schools to close and under what conditions to close or reopen schools are fully removed from the hands of educators, parents, and community.

Within a month of the late-night protest, the United Federation of Teachers (the New York City teachers union) and the NAACP filed *Mulgrew v. Board of Education,* challenging the DOE's lack of public process or democratic accountability for the school closings. Late in March, Manhattan Supreme Court Judge Joan Lobis ruled that "the city failed to follow the new mayoral control law's requirement to fully consider the impact of school closings on students and schools" (Monahan, 2010). A local media headline noted, "Manhattan Supreme Court saved 19 schools, Education department plays musical chairs with new schools" (Monahan, 2010). Judge Lobis nullified the middle-of-the-night vote, finding that the "DOE had failed to adequately disseminate plans for how the existing students would be served if the schools were closed."

The court's decision referenced the generally accepted standard that in the event of a school closing, the chancellor is supposed to prepare an Educational Impact Statement (EIS) that specifies "the impacts of the proposed school closing to any affected students; the ability of other schools in the affected community district to accommodate pupils" (*Mulgrew v. Board of Education, 2010,* p. 3). Judge Lobis found that "it appears to be uncontested that hard copies of the EISs were not provided to parents, nor were they available at the affected schools, or provided to the respective Community Education Councils or School Leadership Teams" (p. 6). Indeed, she concludes, the respondents "failed to provide any meaningful information regarding the impacts on the students or the ability of the schools in the affected community to accommodate those students" (p. 6).

To date, these 19 school closings have been challenged (see Medina, 2010b). However, the future continues to be informed by the poetry and insight of Lowell and Du Bois. While Lobis's decision marks a victory for educators and communities, we must return to the long-festering disaster in many of these schools. David Bloomfield comments on the profound sadness that saturates this turn of events:

> We should rejoice when the judiciary checks illegal use of political authority. . . . But the decision should also be greeted with sadness. That the city should so brazenly violate the letter of the law is contemptible . . . [however,] the DOE plans to let these schools continue to sink, keeping a shell staff and student body for those who didn't get the message that they are passengers on an educational Titanic . . . perhaps aid has been withheld in an intentional, unethical strategy of triage to score political points through headline grabbing closures rather than the slower, less dramatic work required for trust, instructional success. . . . Those are the questions that deserve good faith answers now. (Bloomfield, 2009)

Educational failure has been stated as the primary reason that New York City schools are being closed. This might even be a welcome outcome if educators, youth, and parents were engaged in the decisions to transform schools with structures of accountability to local children and communities. To the contrary, school closing decisions rely heavily on test scores, the exclusion of community and parents, and the silencing of educators. These policies have resulted in a disregard for the future of displaced students, an intensifying suspicion of public officials, and an unleashing of collective and individual dispossession and outrage. We turn now to empirical evidence regarding the consequences of these recent public education policy trends and the pivotal role played by charter expansion in these outcomes.

## A GEOGRAPHY AND ARCHEOLOGY OF DISPOSSESSION: TRACKING THE POLICIES AND THEIR IMPACT

The constellation of political, economic, ideological, and educational forces that come into play in a school closing, or charter opening, needs to be understood with a wide-angle lens of neoliberal policy initiatives, and from the perspective of youth in those communities. Interested in the racialized geography of educational opportunities, Maddy Fox designed Polling for

Justice (PFJ), a participatory, youth-created citywide survey designed to document adolescents' experiences of education, health care, and criminal justice in New York City by race/ethnicity, social class, gender, sexuality, and neighborhood (Fox et al., 2010). Designed in collaboration with a consortium of activist youth organizations, PFJ surveyed more than 1,000 New York City youth about their experiences in schools, with police, and with regard to health care to document the geography and demography of dispossession. This initiative was structured to track where and for whom social policies, institutions, and practices enable and constrict opportunities for youth development across New York City; to capture how youth and adult allies mobilize to resist, negotiate, and challenge collectively these policies and practices; and to create activist scholarship, performances, white papers, organizing brochures, and other forms of evidence to "be of use" in varied organizing campaigns for youth justice and human rights policy struggles.

The rich PFJ database, developed by Brett Stoudt, examines the extent to which *school closings and charter openings map onto zones of dispossession;* that is, to assess the extent to which high dropout/discharge rates are associated with heavy police presence/surveillance/criminalization of youth (a link that the youth researchers emphasized and insisted that we study) and, then, to consider the extent to which these are communities declared educational disasters by the DOE, where schools are being closed and selective admissions/charter schools opened.

By mapping communities with both high dropout/discharge rates and substantial rates of negative youth-police interactions, PFJ identified *zones of dispossession,* communities where substantial public resources are dedicated to policies of intensified testing practices, police surveillance, and school closings. More to the point, we were able to explore neighborhoods where youth of color were being systematically disconnected from educational institutions and, through racial profiling and surveillance, hyperattached to penal institutions. Critically, zones of dispossession are neighborhoods in which public policies systemically push young people (disproportionately young people of color) out of public institutions that cultivate development, inquiry and possibility (e.g., schools) and redirect them into public institutions of containment and control (e.g., prisons, the military). By tracking empirically both the geography and impact of these policies, we can see that policy-based dispossession has a waterfall effect on communities and youth.

A quick review of the maps we were able to create by borough and zip code exposes systematic and predictable patterns of low graduation and high negative police interaction rates, heavily concentrated in a restricted set of zip codes where poor Black and Latino youth are overconcentrated.

Within the boroughs of the Bronx and Brooklyn, many communities are doubly scarred by high dropout/pushout/discharge rates and extensive reporting of negative police interactions. Communities of high school discharge/low graduation rates are also characterized by high rates of youth stops and frisks and high rates of "innocent stops," or stops without arrests (Stoudt, Fox & Fine, 2012). The youth most affected are members of low-income, African American, Latino, and multiethnic groups, with LGBT (lesbian, gay, bisexual, and transgender) youth also disproportionately reporting difficulties with police and in schools.

Once the cross streets for school closings and charter openings were entered into the same database and superimposed on these maps, it was apparent that school closings/charter openings are being located in those communities where pushouts, dropouts, and negative police interaction are most prevalent.

This racialized geography of educational failure and criminal justice involvement, linked with school closings and charter development, lays bare a profound contradiction. While one might argue that schools are being closed to help these communities in desperate need of intervention, the evidence suggests that to the contrary, new institutions are being developed, but not for neighborhood children. New schools open either as charters or with selective admissions criteria, limiting severely the access of neighborhood youth, further constraining their choices and their aspirations.

These deregulatory and exit policies create a profoundly destructive tremor of dislocation destabilizing the grounds of low-income communities, leaving behind the ash of the diminished political power of communities of color and further constricting the life choices of many growing up in poverty. For a moment, we pause to consider the racialized impact of high-stakes testing as the presumed science behind this realignment of educational opportunities.

## MAKING A SCIENCE OF DISPOSSESSION: FOCUS ON TESTING, IGNORE DROPOUT

In Chicago they call it a Renaissance; in New York, a victory for mayoral control. In both instances, without a flood, communities of color experience a deluge of data showered on them, produced by accountability regimes. Testing data have become the self-proclaimed "objective" and "demographically neutral" criteria for school closings, clearing the grounds for charters, contract schools, selective admissions, and privatization. We analyze here, a bit more intensively, the well-funded role of high-stakes testing and accountability regimes as a science of racialized dispossession and then consider why dropout rates—a structural problem of extreme proportions—have been relatively neglected in the discourse of educational accountability and in the selling of charters.

## The National Problem

An overview of the national testing landscape reveals that youth of color, those living in poverty, and immigrant youth are disproportionately likely to attend schools that require passage of standardized tests in order to graduate (even if these students have completed and passed all required courses), more likely to fail these exams and leave school prior to graduation, and far more likely to *endure the lifelong cumulative penalties of diploma denial and structural racism* (Darling-Hammond, 2010b; Glass, 2008; Zhao, 2009).

According to the Center on Education Policy, as of 2010, 26 states currently have or are planning mandatory exit exams. Exit exams are more prevalent in states with higher percentages of Black and Hispanic students, as well as states with the highest degrees of poverty and in cities with high rates of ninth-grade retention, low graduation rates, high incidence of discharges and dropouts, younger students in GED programs, and increased dropout/pushout rates for English language learners (ELLs), Blacks, and Latino students (Center on Educational Policy, 2010). If Black and Latino youth are more likely to have to pass exit exams in order to graduate, they are also more likely to drop out when these exams are required or the testing produces failure. (For a detailed discussion of the racial impact of high-stakes testing, see Center for Educational Policy, 2009, 2010; Darling-Hammond, 2010b; Fine et al., 2009.)

In a 2000 report, *High Stakes Testing and High School Completion,* Marguerite Clarke, Walter Haney, and George Madaus of the National Board on Educational Testing and Public Policy concluded that high-stakes testing does, indeed, increase dropout rates—although they note that there is room for further study to determine exactly how this relationship works.

While many factors contribute to dropout, the insidious role of high-stakes testing has been documented by scholars studying experiences of student attrition in many contexts including, but not limited to, the "Texas miracle," English language learners, underresourced schools, and schools with high concentrations of students of color (Valenzuela, 2004). Let us consider the case of New York state.

Despite promises of accountability and a mantra of "civil rights," high-stakes testing has been associated with a variety of well documented adverse effects (cheating, tracking, segregation, substantial economic cost)—especially critical to this analysis are school closings and increased dropout rates among youth of color. The links between high stakes testing and dropout—or what is increasingly called diploma denial (see Fine & Ruglis, 2007)—are becoming more explicit in New York state, where students in the graduating class of 2012 will be required to pass five tests to earn a high school diploma. Jennifer Medina, an education writer for *The New York Times,* tells us, "If the new standards had been in place for the class of 2009, the city's graduation rate would have been roughly 45%, instead of the nearly 60% that city officials boasted of . . . among Black and Latino students, barely more than one third would have qualified for diplomas" (2010b, p. A16).

The racialized impact of high-stakes testing has a long history, exposed by Horace Mann Bond in the 1950s, to the present day. And yet evidence of disparate impact does not seem sufficiently compelling for policy-makers to shift gears and slow the accelerating reliance on high-stakes testing, or to lower the stakes. The commitment to testing seems far more fixed than the commitment to educating and graduating all children. Indeed, standardized tests are today the basis for determining students' promotion and graduation, teacher evaluations, school success, and the conditions for school closings as well as chapter openings. High-stakes testing has become the science of dispossession—enabling, legitimating, and yet obscuring the real crisis: the severe, racialized rates of school dropouts.

## THE DROPOUT EPIDEMIC

There is, indeed, a real and denied structural crisis of miseducation, evident, in part, through the dramatically racialized dropout rates that characterize urban America. In 2006, the Bill and Melinda Gates Foundation funded a study entitled *The Silent Epidemic* in which they claim that:

> There is a high school dropout epidemic in America. Each year, almost one third of all public high school students—and nearly one half of all blacks, Hispanics, and Native Americans—fail to graduate from public high school with their class. Many of these students abandon school with less than two years to complete their high school education. This tragic cycle has not substantially improved during the past few decades when education reform has been high on the public agenda. During this time, the public has been almost entirely unaware of the severity of the dropout problem due to inaccurate data. The consequences remain tragic. (Bridgeland, DiIulio, & Morison, 2006; see also Fine & Ruglis, 2008)

A year later, the Alliance for Excellent Education published "The High Cost of High School Dropouts" and found that if students who dropped out in the class of 2007 graduated, the national economy would have secured $329 billion in income earned over their lifetimes (Cook & Tashlik, 2005). While the alarms of dropout crisis populate the headlines and national white papers, there has been surprisingly scant attention paid to the dropout crisis within the charter movement and, consistent with this point, little systematic research on this question. Let us consider for a moment the scope of the dropout crisis and its racialized distributions and then return to the odd silence within the charter movement.

The existing literature on the dropout problem marks numerous points of agreement among progressive and conservative researchers.

While strategies for calculating precise dropout rates are contested, scholars and policy analysts across the political spectrum agree that the rates are high, racialized, and most acute in central cities for students attending "dropout factories." There is consensus that the rates are disproportionately high so for African American, Latino, and youth living in poverty (Fine & Ruglis, 2008).

Drawing from an updated version of Fine and Ruglis (2008), we summarize below the disparate outcomes for young people without high school degrees as compared to those who are at least high school graduates. Comparisons are made on the basis of academic well-being, likelihood of employment, income, access to health insurance, physical health, criminal justice involvement, parenting, voting, paying taxes, community engagement, and mental health outcomes (see summary in Table 5.1; Fine & Ruglis, 2008). To be clear, there are enormous personal, social, and collective economic costs of social policies that diminish the likelihood of high school graduation in the poorest communities of color.

To complicate matters, the negative outcomes of dropouts are far worse for African American and Latino young adults than for Whites without a diploma. For every indicator listed in Table 5.1, African American and Latino youth without high school diplomas experience substantially more negative consequences than their White peers. Structural racism accelerates the negative impact of diploma denial.

There is substantial agreement on the dropout problem as a threat to our national public health (Ruglis & Freudenberg, 2010), and yet, surprisingly, there is nothing in the ideology or available empirical evidence that suggests that charters offer a strategy to reduce dropout rates. In fact, not even a promise and little research.

TABLE 5.1. The Impact of Diploma Denial

| Diploma Denial Consequence Sectors | Evidence |
|---|---|
| Economic impact | Young adults without high school diplomas are more likely to be unemployed, underemployed, discouraged workers and earn far less than college-educated peers.<br>These trends are exacerbated for Black and Latino young adults without diplomas. |
| Health impact | Every year of education has positive health consequences in terms of coronary health disease, blood pressure, teen pregnancy, diabetes, obesity, and asthma. |
| Criminal-justice impact | Young women and men without high school diplomas are substantially more likely to be imprisoned than those with diplomas and some college; the odds of ending up in the criminal justice system are substantially greater for African American pushouts than for Whites.<br>While diploma penalty affects all demographic groups in terms of incarceration, Pettit and Western (2004) document that the cumulative risk of death or incarceration (by ages 20 to 34) is approximately six times higher for African American men without a high school diploma than for Whites. |
| Opportunities for protective parenting | Mothers without high school diplomas are more likely to be raising children in communities where the youth are vulnerable to violence and police harassment, and are worried about health/finances/housing. |

## CONCLUSION

In the end, the educational advancement of African American people cannot be solely measured by the extent to which *some* African American children are able to have a middle class home and schooling experience—almost in a "talented tenth" sense with the notion that they will reach back and help those at the bottom. Instead, it can be best measured by the extent to which *African American children at the bottom* are provided the social and educational means to elevate themselves [emphasis added]. (Morris, 2009, pp. 157–159)

In New Orleans, Chicago, and New York City, as throughout the nation, dispossession is foundational to inequality, animated policies of deregulation and exit carved very precisely and with a very sharp edge, around the contours of race, ethnicity, and class—ironically in the name of educational accountability and public safety. In contrast to Jerome Morris's call for educational transformation in which "children at the bottom are provided the economic, social, and educational means to elevate themselves," today we witness a series of regressive educational policies in motion. These policies are proceeding without community, parent, educator, or youth consultation in ways that produce private profit and consolidation of corporate—not community—power; advocating strategies despite evidence of ineffectiveness and disparate impact; accelerating disinvestment and growing inequalities disproportionately affecting poor students of color. In sum, these policies are leaving most low-income children of color behind in terms of achievement, opportunity, and graduation rates.

Designed as if responsive to pain, fear, anxiety, and a hunger for educational accountability, these policies (based, for example, on high-stakes testing) exacerbate already wide opportunity gaps by race and class, laying the groundwork for school closings and charter/contract school openings. Communities lose key institutions and democratic processes are undermined; local leaders are ignored as new drive-by educational entrepreneurs can be found in abundance.

As we have noted throughout, the very schools in question are, no doubt, in deep trouble. Closing them and reopening the schools as charters or traditional schools with selective admissions or private, contracted schools for populations of youth outside the neighborhoods affected by school closure policy, however, fails to address the persistent and deepening crisis for the very poorest students of color attending the schools being shut down. While individual charters may serve some children well, charters as national policy are exploited today as a decoy for disinvestment and the profound, intensifying neglect of the poorest students of color.

As we learn from New Orleans, Chicago, and New York, it is important to ask, To what extent do contemporary public policies and proposed reform strategies address the long-standing educational crisis of miseducation and dropout or dispossession *in collaboration with community, educators, and youth to narrow* the inequality gaps? Conversely, to what extent do contemporary public policies and new structures align ideologically with corporate interests in ways that *widen* opportunity gaps, increase the incarceration rates, swell the rates of diploma denial, and perhaps most generally, intensify dislocation and dispossession for very poor students of color?

We are concerned that the reckless act of widening the inequality gaps already plaguing urban America and eroding what we know as the public sector facilitates a new private-sector educational order— a radically restructured system increasingly emphasizing capitalization of public assets and ever-greater concentration of diminished education resources for those whom conservatives consider the "cognitive elite" (Gottfredson, 2004).

# CHAPTER 6

# Reclaiming "Public": Deepening National Commitments to Public Investment and Public Innovation

We live in an era of disaster capitalism, structural racism, and huge inequality gaps. Authors as disparate as Paul Krugman, Naomi Klein, Manning Marable, and David Harvey have discussed a relationship between crisis and political opportunity. Paul Krugman has noted that the recent fiscal crisis is being used by the Right to push an even more ambitious but, ultimately, similar agenda:

> So here's the reality: America's fiscal reality over the next few years isn't bad. We do have a serious long run budget problem, which will have to be resolved with a combination of health care reform and other measures, probably including a moderate rise in taxes. But we should ignore those who pretend to be concerned with fiscal responsibility, but whose real goal is to dismantle the welfare state—and are trying to use crises everywhere to frighten us into giving them what they want. (Krugman, 2010)

The constant drumbeat of "crisis" in public education, announced with a parade of racialized images of academic deficit, has been used as a lever to introduce various forms of privatization, including charter choice, into public school systems. Federal policy has followed corporate lead. The question before us remains, are charter schools likely to fix what ails? The preliminary evidence is unconvincing and the political dynamics suspect.

## NEW JERSEY: THE BUDGET CRISIS AND PUBLIC EDUCATION

With a new governor promising to slash public expenditures, in 2010, New Jersey declared a budget crisis and transformed the state education system. Refusing to tax the wealthiest residents of the state or fund the

TABLE 6.1. The Binary Tradeoffs and Discourse of Charter Reform

| Challenges | Charter Campaign Solution | Strategic Investment Strategies |
|---|---|---|
| How to create more "good" schools? | Competition | Develop learning cultures by engaging parents, encouraging creativity among youth, and supporting and increasing educator capacity. |
| How to support low-income children seeking quality education? | Support their exit from local schools and communities | Nurture strong partnerships among educators, community, and youth to rebuild public schools as vital resources in community development. |
| How should we as a nation support innovative schools? | Low public investment/ high private investment | Strategic public investment in public education. |
| Who should have access to a quality education? | Those students who are best equipped to use the opportunity well; low-need students | All children deserve access to quality local schools—including, but not limited to, students with complex learning needs and including, but not limited to, English language learners, students with special needs, and youth released from juvenile facilities. |
| How do we hold ourselves accountable? | Market our exemplars; flood the zone with critical attacks on public education; blame unions; rely upon test scores for student and teacher evaluation/humiliation, and school report cards and as the basis of school closings and opening public sites for charter development | Build multipronged accountability systems that assess students' academic work through rich, local performance assessments that encourage students to write, inquire critically, engage with music, art, and community life, and to develop rich and active knowledge about the disciplines. Stop the overreliance on testing and the policing and punishment of youth and educators. Create multiple pathways to graduation. Hold districts and states accountable in terms of finance equity, adequacy, and support for public schools. Promote meaningful ways to educate youth about their collective responsibilities and voice within a multiracial democracy and build communities of critically engaged citizens. |

state educational formula, the economic, then political, and then educational "crisis" was born. It was within this context that the expansion of charters was promoted as the policy strategy of choice for fixing public education.

The charter movement in New Jersey, especially Newark, represents a tight fit with ideological predispositions of the moment inasmuch as it is financed not by new public dollars but, rather, by a strategic redirection of money away from more traditional public schools, a triaging of a selective cohort of children to charters, and a diversionary turn away from the large and difficult task of public education. Consistent with this point, charter schools have been excluded from the most recent round of budget cutting in a cross-section of states, including New Jersey. While public school districts have been cut by $820 million in state aid, the charter schools remain flat, relatively immune to the budget crisis.

We take you, for a moment, to Trenton, March 2010:

> Two days after introducing a budget that cut $820 million in education aid, the governor came out swinging against teachers unions he said have been flush with cash yet are still demanding raises for their members while private sector employees endure pay cuts or layoffs. He called on the unions to give back or forestall raises granted in new contracts and enlisted the help of charter schools in demonstrating [that] quality education does not have to drain a municipal or state budget. "You are the masters of doing more with less because you have been consistently underfunded by the statute that was passed to establish you," Christie said. To help keep down the cost of education, Christie said, public school teachers should forego their raises, contribute to the cost of their health care and contribute a market-based share of their pension. Earlier in the day, Education Commissioner Bret Schundler told the same crowd that funding for New Jersey's charter schools is expected to remain flat next year, requiring school officials to work cooperatively with their public counterparts and rein in increasing health benefits and salary packages. (Spoto, 2010)

Since that time, Christie has declared New Jersey's public education system a "failure," although national, and state-level data defy Christie's assessment. Whether we rely on NAEP scores or graduation rates, New Jersey scores among the top five states in the nation. Nevertheless, crisis has been declared while the need for increased strategic investment in public education is ignored. New public resources will not be poured into public education, although there is legislation to invest state funds into parochial and private schools via a voucher bill.

Reform most powerfully reflected in charters is represented as simply a matter of reengineering school systems on the basis of choice with essentially fixed budgets. Charters as a highly circumscribed experimental prod to stimulate innovation accompanied with new targeted resources for neighborhood schools would conceivably represent at least part of a plausible alternate strategy for reinventing public education. Unfortunately, the necessary fulcrum for education reform, strategic investment, has essentially disappeared. Instead, the emphasis is on cost-neutral charter investments, deregulation of public schooling, promotion of student exit, reemergence of voucher plans, and blatant disregard for empirical data either on the front end or back end of policy-making.

Braided with this political strategy, there is a media strategy. Newspapers, magazines, talk radio, and now film would have us believe that innovation is not possible outside the market. The insidious role of high-stakes tests—as the "scientific" basis upon which students' promotion and graduation, access to selective schools, school report cards, teacher evaluations, school closings, and charter openings—requires much more critical scrutiny than we can provide here. Suffice it to say, publishing houses, testing companies, textbook companies, and measurement organizations are profiting as children of color and poverty are being redlined out of their public schools, and communities are losing control over their local schools.

If the dismantling of public education has not been the explicit motive for the full charter movement, it certainly has been among its consequences. As stated by Amy Stuart Wells (2009):

> Charter school reform . . . mirrors, and often exacerbates, the broader conditions of inequality in the society as a whole. . . . My central argument is that charter schools are not the cause of the rampant inequality in the field of education and the society at large; they are merely a symptom of the now-prevalent narrow and illogical thinking about how public policy might help us solve this inequality. (pp. 156, 157)

Importantly, these dynamics exacerbate the growing inequalities that pervade and pervert economic and racial formations in the United States.

## THE BINARY TRADEOFFS OF CHARTER POLICY

Clearly, we are critical of any single reform initiative that purports to heal all that ails public education. This is especially the case when, for example, charter school advocates fail to address the historic racial and class inequities of government underinvestment in the poorest school districts; do not argue for increased targeted public allocations, jobs, housing, or health care; and are not developing programs on the basis of what can be empirically validated as having worked in the past. At the moment the public debate regarding education policy and, more specifically, charter schooling has largely been driven by business or private-sector frames for determining policy intervention, the targets of such reform, and how to examine impact. This section is intended to distill much of the binary underpinnings of the charter movement's advocacy position. Our intention is to explicate and challenge these binaries articulated and circulated by charter advocates.

## Competition, Not Collaboration

A primary argument of the charter movement is that public education systems/bureaucracies have failed because of the absence of competition and that competition will spur innovation. In the marketplace this has resulted in wealth expansion and increased income for some, and widened inequality gaps for us all. In the education marketplace the same dynamics are expected to produce increased academic performance. Within this context compelling evidence regarding the centrality of collaboration, professional communities, and the relationship of family-school partnerships to academic performance is simply not considered. Two sorts of empirical evidence have been neglected: evidence that challenges the relation of competition to equitable achievement and evidence that recognizes the significance of collaboration to academic success.

## Reallocation or Investment of Resources in Public Education

An essential promise of charter reform is that it can deliver better results for the same money as public education—or for less. Present policy focuses on reallocating fixed and most recently declining public dollars from traditional schools to charters. The problem is defined not as one of level of investment but rather of inefficient and ineffective allocations of scarce dollars. However, recent data indicate that the difficulties and failures of public education in the poorest communities of color can in large part be traced to unequal investment of public dollars across affluent and impoverished communities and the cascading of problems attendant to poverty—racism, housing insecurity, mass incarceration, and immigration that disrupts families. The present policy debate rarely if ever surfaces the essential questions about the impact of the inequality gaps on learning and the impact of unequal investment by race and class.

## Equitable or Differential Access to a Charter Education

Although charter schools are primarily located in the poorest communities of color, equitable access is a persistent problem. Charter advocates would argue that the rationing of such access is a consequence of the scarcity of charters relative to traditional public schools rather than specific gate-keeping practices. The empirical evidence argues otherwise. Data across state lines indicate that charter schools, in the aggregate, admit and retain easy-to-educate youth, that is, relatively effective, disciplined students, while simultaneously denying access to the most challenging learners. The evidence regarding differences between charter and traditional schools on their percentage of English as a Second Language and special education students is striking. Equally important, lottery admission to charters by definition draws parents most committed to identifying and securing new educational options for their children. In turn, parental norms regarding the value of education are more likely shared by charter students than the larger pool of students attending traditional public schools from similar neighborhoods. Finally, the charter practice of removing underperforming or misbehaving students and returning them to their public schools is another source of filtering. The systematic filtering of learners into and out of charters helps to burnish the social myth of greater effectiveness.

## Marketing Exemplar Performance or Documenting the Complexities of Quality Education for All

Charter reform momentum can be traced to many factors. One of the most powerful contributors has been the repeated media saga of the exemplary charter making profound differences in the lives of very poor students of color. This narrative has been threaded through the experience of individual charters in Harlem, Washington, DC, and Chicago and, most recently, through the film *Waiting for Superman*. It has also been offered as evidence of policy success, thus legitimating expansion. However, these narratives do not offer a basis for shaping either policy direction or expansion. To the contrary, policy change needs to be informed by systematic data collection that rigorously examines not exemplary experience but rather the more general impact of a reform. Exemplary performance cannot answer that question. And yet we continue to trade in the evidence of the exemplar rather than aggregated performance in selling charter policy.

## Implementing an Effective Reform Agenda for Academic and Community Development: Simple or Complex

Educational entrepreneurs and charter advocates have indicated that the work of transforming public education is relatively simple. Spin-off new schools unencumbered by public bureaucracy, and in the new education marketplace ever more effective learning environments will be produced. The parents' freedom to choose, staff's enlarged prospect for innovation as schools move outside the shadow of bureaucratic regulation, and intensifying competition are expected to cohere and cleanse as well as reinvent public education. This is a relatively simple, market-driven formula for change. But what if the situation is more complex than imagined? For example, how can school deregulation address the array of complex factors associated with the churning of teachers in public schools that, in turn, influences decline in student performance? How can schools suffering from the spreading virus of disinvestment support youth who are contending with the devastating impact of a recession, budget cuts, and a wide range of policy-based troubles including housing and economic insecurity, police harassment, unemployment, mass incarceration, and in some communities deportation, incorporated into this market model of public education?

There is much to be learned from school-community transformation projects dotting the country, all quite different and bold. But this much is true across settings—any experimental public education change project requires that these complex questions, and the financing of an ambitious experiment, be consciously, collectively and critically addressed if an effective architecture for public education reform is to be developed and implemented. Alternatively, if reform architecture is built on the soft sand of simple nostrum that market formula will heal public education, it will almost certainly collapse in on itself, leaving behind the communities most in need.

Simple binaries work effectively as an ideological distraction and a media flash point, but ultimately undermine the complex, demanding work necessary to rebuild public education. Fortunately, alternate approaches to the national project of public education and democracy, in urban communities, seem to be brewing. Below we consider two images of public innovation borne from community struggle joined with educator commitment and strategic investment.

## PROVOCATIVE IMAGES OF PUBLIC INNOVATION

Mexican American parents in Little Village in Chicago and the Asian American parents in Chinatown in Philadelphia probably didn't talk to each other, but they shared a problem. In these distinct communities—joined by poverty and the riches of strong immigrant families—they wanted a local public school that would appreciate and cultivate their rich cultural heritage, linguistic diversity, and histories of struggle. They wanted a school that would honor the arts and the more traditional areas of academic pursuit; they wanted a school that grew from the wisdom and heritages they held so dear that would offer their children resources as they planned for futures of meaning, engagement, college, work, and contributing to community life. More to the point, they wanted a learning experience for their children that was richly complex and that joined their past to a future. Their aspiration was to create a public education that joined group culture to democratic citizenship, technical learning to critical thinking, and career to an appreciation for the arts as an incubator germinating social justice commitment, imagination, and creation.

The Little Village neighborhood sits in Chicago's Southwest Side. In 1995, members of the Little Village community engaged political and grassroots organizing to pressure Chicago Public Schools (CPS) for a high school to address issues of overcrowding. Elected officials asked community members to register their concerns through official CPS channels. When that didn't work, on Mother's Day, May 13, 17 members of the Little Village community launched a hunger strike. They drank water and juice for 19 days, camping out in cold and rainy weather, in a vacant plot of land across from a demolished cooking oil factory.

Due to national media coverage and substantial support throughout the city, CPS decided to approach negotiations with community members from Little Village. *The Chicago Sun-Times* reports the victory:

> Seven years after the first promises were made, the new Little Village/Lawndale High School Campus opens Tuesday At a cost of $63 million, it's the most expensive Chicago public school building ever built, with a swimming pool, two gyms, a distance-learning lab and a small day care. Its architecture pays tribute to Mexican culture and is packed with reminders of the hunger strike, including a massive sundial that highlights the 19-day fast. (Grossman, 2005)

Four schools are housed in the structure: (1) visual and performing arts, (2) math, science, and technology, (3) world languages, and (4) social justice. All of them opened in the summer of 2005. Remembering the spirit of the hunger strikers and the deep participation of elders and young, the schools are organized around history, youth inquiry, and critical pedagogy. An educator at the Social Justice High School describes students' appetite for critical history, learning about the near-genocide of the Native Americans by European colonizers and the murder of union leaders by the U.S. government in the early 1900s. He noted, "I think they're hungry for it. Deep in their consciousness they have a lot of questions about it, based on their experiences in a community that's marginalized" (Cardinale, 2009, p. 2).

Seven hundred and sixty miles to the east, parents and community members in Chinatown, Philadelphia, were meeting to create a new small elementary school. The Folk Arts-Cultural Treasures Charter School website explains:

> The Folk Arts-Cultural Treasures Charter School in Philadelphia, FACT, was born out of years of Asian American parental dissatisfaction with the Philadelphia public schools. Philadelphia's Chinatown had no school—with none being planned. The nonprofit group Asian Americans United filed a lawsuit against the district and eventually decided to create a multi-racial diverse school. Today students of Chinese, Vietnamese, Cambodian, Laotian and Hmong heritage study together in a curriculum steeped in respect for language, culture and arts. The school integrates artists, storytellers, dancers and musicians into the daily curriculum, satisfying community developed "folk standards" as rigorous and perhaps more engaging than "state academic standards." With a rich set of linguistic resources, educators work closely with families and community, often through translators.
>
> All students at FACTS have the opportunity to study with master folk-artists, like an African storyteller or Tibetan sand artist. Folk Arts provides students with an opportunity to more fully immerse themselves in their own culture while being exposed to the cultures of their neighbors. By the time they graduate, students are more likely to be ready to participate in a diverse and dynamic democracy as engaged and responsible people.
>
> FACTS serves over 400 students from a cross section of Philadelphia neighborhoods, committed to a community-based and intergenerational vision of learning where parents, other family members, elders and the community sit at the center of the schools' design. (FACTS Web site, http://www.factschool.org/home)

In both Chicago and Philadelphia, parents and community mobilized for rich education that would engage their children with dignity, welcome parents and community elders as resources, and develop in their students the academic and civic tools necessary for lives of meaningful, creative, and critical participation in public life. Educators and community built these schools with an intention to create complex learning environments of intellectual rigor, community wisdom and deep participation. Over time, these schools have blossomed into resources for community cultural development. It is precisely this kind of innovation and public education that the poorest communities of color deeply desire and deserve. It is of course time for this kind of critical and complex innovation to be foundational to public education—not an exception.

We hear from public school educators that today, only a few years later, traditional public schools are being denied opportunities to innovate as Little Village and FACT were able to do. Communities are exiled from the praxis of educational reform; educators are treated like widgets; the myopic focus on testing is suffocating innovation and desire while charters are being coopted into a larger campaign to undermine communities of color, de-professionalize educators, deny youth critical pedagogy, and deregulate public education. And yet the voices of resistance are mounting.

## TOWARD A NEW CONSENSUS:
## THE INCREASING CALL FOR INVESTMENT
## TO SPUR INNOVATION AND FOSTER EFFECTIVE SCHOOLING

The spring of 2010 turned out to be a politically depressing season with the economic recession and budget crises creating profound forms of strain. In the seams of this political economic rupture, however, an alternate frame for improving the performance of public education became increasingly visible. In May 2010, the National Council of Churches Governing Board (2010), a religious group of 36 Christian communities with a combined membership of 45 million persons in more than 100,000 congregations across the United States, unanimously adopted a position on public education that called for:

> Public education, publicly funded, universally available and accountable to the public while imperfect is essential for all children that are served. Instruments of the marketplace are not appropriate tools for educating children. (2010, p.1)

Regarding charter schools, the letter states:

> Federal policy today is encouraging states to rapidly expand choice through charter schools. We are concerned when we hear the civil rights to education

being redefined as the right to school choice . . . for we know that equitable access to opportunity is more difficult to achieve in a mass of privatized alternatives to traditional public schools or in school districts being carved into a small schools of choice. . . . Our energies should be directed at the traditional public schools that the majority of our children will attend.

On balance we believe that democratic operations of our public schools is our best hope for ensuring that families can secure the services to which their children have a right . . . we believe that if government invests in charter schools that report to private boards, government, not the vicissitudes of the marketplace, should be expected to provide the oversight to the common good. (National Council of Churches Governing Board, 2010, p. 2)

Two months later, in July 2010, a wide-ranging group of civil rights organizations released the Framework for Providing All Students an Opportunity to Learn through Reauthorization of the Elementary and Secondary Education Act. "As a community of civil rights organizations, we believe that access to a high quality education is a fundamental civil right." They outlined six principles to "protect every child's civil right to a high-quality education":

- equitable opportunities for all
- utilization of systematically proven and effective educational methods
- public and community engagement in education reforms
- safe and educationally sound learning environments
- diverse learning environments
- comprehensive and substantive accountability systems to maintain equitable opportunities and high outcomes (Lawyers Committee for Civil Rights and Law, 2010, p. 1)

Like the letter from religious communities, the civil rights document supports academic standards "by ensuring sufficient resources to address extreme state budget cuts and interstate inequities" (Lawyers Committee for Civil Rights and Law, 2010, p. 2). They are unwilling to advocate for standards without redressing gross material inequities that litter the landscape of public education. At the same time the document underscores the need to rely on empirical data to guide policy development be it choice of pedagogy, structuring of learning culture, or supports necessary to develop effective teachers. Importantly, they reject the notion that Race to the Top, as a competitive effort, will help all children, and they recommend instead a "shift from competitive grants for a few states to incentives for all states to embrace systemic reform" (Lawyers Committee for Civil Rights and Law, 2010, p. 3).

To the question of school failure, they argue for reinventing low-performing schools as community schools. Familiar with the adverse consequences of school closings, they caution that school closure should be a last resort, deployed with appropriate safeguards. (See also the Broader, Bolder Approach to Education website, www.boldapproach.org/statement.html.)

Most critically, on the significant policy shift from traditional to charter schools, this distinguished group of civil rights organizations writes:

> While charters can serve as laboratories for innovation, we are concerned about the overrepresentation of charter schools in low income and predominantly minority communities. There is no evidence that charter operators are systematically more effective in creating higher student outcomes nationwide. . . . Thus, while some charter schools can and do work for some students, they are not a universal solution for systemic change for all students, especially those with the highest needs. (Lawyers Committee for Civil Rights and Law, 2010, pp. 8–9)

Any commitment to *public innovation* requires significant strategic investment in educational policies, public schools, and community-based projects that explicitly address inequality gaps, structural racism, and inequitable opportunities. Anything less is part of a conscious or unconscious policy charade likely to further coarsen discourse regarding education policy, misdirect public attention away from the issues undermining effective schooling, and contribute to the escalating nihilistic belief that public education must be abandoned if we are save it. And so we address now two critical policy questions:

1.   Does money matter?
2.   How can charter schools be fully public?

## Does Money Matter? An Argument for Strategic Investment

While hotly debated, there is a direct and strong relationship between strategic investment in public education and academic outcomes. For the question, Does Money Matter? the evidence is quite clear. *While money doesn't guarantee improved outcomes, inadequate money guarantees poor achievement.* Strategic investment matters. Adequate and equitable education, as an enactment of democracy, comes at a price.

Let us turn first to the question of inequity, drawing on the writings of epidemiologists Wilkerson and Pickett, who argue convincingly with global data on the adverse impact of inequality gaps. "We know that inequality affects so many outcomes, across so much of society. The transformation of our society is a project in which we all have a shared interest. Greater equality is the gateway to a society capable of improving the quality of life for all of us and an essential step in the development of a sustainable economic system" (Wilkerson & Pickett, 2010, p. 232).

Inequitable investment in education results in large differences in graduation rates, academic achievement, and even test scores. This common sense relationship has been too frequently obfuscated by marketplace ideology, which contends that choice can substitute for public investment, money doesn't matter, and "no excuses" are acceptable. It is within this context that Linda Darling-Hammond notes:

> International studies continue to confirm that the US educational system is also one of the most unequal in terms of inputs. In contrast to European and Asian nations that fund schools centrally and equally, the wealthiest school districts in the US spend nearly 10 times more than the poorest districts, and spending ratios of 3:1 are common within states. . . . This creates huge inequalities in educational outcomes that ultimately weaken the very fabric of our nation. . . .
>
> Recent analysis, of data prepared for school equity cases in more than 20 states has found that on every tangible measure—from qualified teachers and class size to textbooks, computers, facilities and curriculum offerings—schools serving larger numbers of students of color have significantly fewer resources than schools serving more affluent White students. (2010a, p. 12)

It is on this basis that the United States placed 29th on the most recent international standardized-testing rankings in science and 35th in math out of 40 nations. What is rarely discussed in relationship to these scores is that the United States is "among those [nations] where two students of different economic backgrounds have the largest difference in expected scores. On this measure of equity, the US ranks 45th out of 55 countries, just above Brazil and Mexico." Thus, Darling-Hammond concludes that "the United States' poor [academic] standing is largely a product of unequal access for underserved students of color to the kinds of intellectually challenging learning measured on these international assessments" (Darling-Hammond, 2010a, p. 12).

During eras of substantial federal investment, the achievement gaps between Blacks and Whites have narrowed. Darling-Hammond explains how investment pays off, using international, historic, and state-by-state analyses:

> Driven by the belief that equal educational opportunity was a national priority, the Elementary and Secondary Education Act of 1965 targeted resources

to communities with the most need, recognizing that where a child grows should not determine where he or she ends up. . . . Efforts to level the playing field for children were supported by intensive investments in bringing and keeping talented individuals in teaching, improving teacher education and investing in research and development.

These investments began to pay off in measurable ways. By the mid 1970s, gaps in educational attainment had closed substantially. Improvements in educational achievement for students of color followed. In reading large gains in Black students' performance throughout the 1970s and early 1980s reduce[d] the achievement gap considerably, cutting it nearly in half in just 15 years. The achievement gap in mathematics also narrowed sharply between 1973 and 1986. Financial aid for higher education was sharply increased, especially for need based scholarships and loads. For a brief period in the mid 1970s, Black and Hispanic students were attending college at rates comparable to those of Whites.

However, this optimistic vision of equal and expanding educational opportunities, along with the gains from the "Great Society" programs, was later pushed back. Most targeted federal programs supporting investments in college access and K–12 schools in urban and poor rural areas were reduced or eliminated during the Reagan administration in 1980s. (2010a, p. 20)

Over time, federal investment in education slipped from 12% of funding to 6% during the 1980s. Urban schools deteriorated with drops in per-pupil expenditures, tax cuts, and growing enrollments of "high need" children. According to Darling-Hammond, after 1988, the reading achievement gap grew sharply and by 2005, the average "Black or Hispanic twelfth grader was reading at the level for the average White eighth grader" (p. 21).

As Darling-Hammond has further demonstrated with her case analysis of the Abbott districts in New Jersey, poor communities of color bolstered by a state judicial decision requiring equitable, strategic investment in education, have enjoyed significant improvement in academic achievement. She provides a detailed response to the question, "Does strategic investment matter?"

Many people have looked to examples like Finland and Singapore for clues about how to take a low-achieving and inequitable system and dramatically transform outcomes for all students and schools. But there are also examples here at home. One example of how strategic investments can produce systemic improvement can be found in New Jersey. Most are familiar with the Abbott decisions that have come out of the legal cases initially launched in the 1960s. But the real legacy of Abbott is the set of systemic changes recently made in P-12 education across the state, providing an extraordinary leap in equity and opportunity that has propelled New Jersey to one of the top-achieving states in the nation and dramatically reduced the achievement gap between white students and their black and Hispanic peers. (Darling Hammond, 2010a, pp. 14–15)

First, state aid brought per-pupil revenue in the 28 (later 30) Abbott districts up to the per-pupil expenditures in the state's 110 successful, suburban districts. Previously, districts serving most of the state's African American and Hispanic students had spent about half of what wealthy districts like Princeton spent.

With $246 million in parity aid, coupled with $312 million in supplemental program assistance, New Jersey developed a new state curriculum linked to state standards. These dollars were designed to support whole-school reform, ensure early childhood education for 3- and 4-year olds taught by a highly qualified teaching force, create full-day kindergarten, and enable smaller class sizes. The new resources also allowed for greater investment in classroom technology, facilities and social services, and summer programs to help students catch up. Finally, it supported extensive professional development, new urban teacher education programs, and literacy programs that brought classroom libraries and expert literacy coaches to inner-city schools. Most importantly, these dollars equalized the system, seeking to close the resource and opportunity gaps between the haves and have-nots.

From Abbott, we learned that real improvement does not happen overnight. Many urban districts struggled at first. Presently, New Jersey is arguably the highest-achieving state in the nation. It has cut its achievement gap in half over the last decade, and its African American and Hispanic students outscore the average student in California. The results speak for themselves. Today, New Jersey, a state where 45% of students are of color, ranks first in the nation in writing performance on NAEP and among the top five states in every other subject area—competing neck-and-neck with states that have many fewer low-income students of color.

All these accomplishments occurred in a strong teacher-union state, a factor that the charter movement has identified as a toxin to meaningful reform. The reform experience in New Jersey, however, belies the highly charged, ideological, and ultimately self-interested assertion that unions impede student achievement. To the contrary, in New Jersey, teachers were active participants in the solution, shaping the strategy and sharing in the successes.

States like New Jersey are proof positive that we cannot settle only for individual school-based reforms and changes. If we are to truly turn around our nation's 5,000 lowest-performing schools, we need systemic change that focuses on the development of highly competent teaching in reasonably funded, supportive school environments. We need to organize around ambitious learning goals evaluated with high-quality assessments. Critically, we need to support all of these action steps with the resources necessary for successful implementation. We cannot improve thousands of schools on a case-by-case basis. We need a systematic approach, like that in high-achieving nations, that offers real, lasting improvements to each and every one of those schools.

Indeed, if money didn't matter, wealthy communities would easily sacrifice their fiscal advantage. Money matters, and strategic investment matters too.

Once the question of money is settled, a second policy question needs to be addressed: If strategic investment were our primary federal and state policy framework, resting on values of equity and deep accountability, under what conditions would charter schools simply be an element of public innovation?

## Critical Considerations for Keeping Charters Public

In this frenzied, increasingly polarized environment, the question that remains unasked by policy makers and the electorate is, What are the fundamental obligations of a publicly funded institution such as schools to a wider citizenry? What makes a public school public and, more precisely, what makes a public charter school public?

Charter reform is a case example of a social policy structured to neglect the fundamental obligation of every publicly funded institution to remain accountable to the citizenry financing its work, accessible to those in need of its services, and just in allocating resources across race and class divides. The claim that charter schools are a public good, however, has little if any legitimacy unless it is tethered to rigorous legislative accountability and enforcement demands. It is within this context that New York state and New Jersey have promulgated legislation that requires charter schools to meet new standards of transparency in reporting the academic performance of students, financial management of public funds, and equity of access for the most learning challenged students.

In the spring of 2010, the New York state legislature deliberated over more than doubling the number of charter schools (Medina, 2010a). Charter lobbyists, hedge-fund advocates, and charter school parents advanced an agenda of rapid expansion absent additional state regulations or obligations. Alternatively, the state union for teachers, NYSUT, proposed that any expansion of charter schooling had to be accompanied by a mandate to make them more publicly accountable to the state, the communities where they are situated, and learning-challenged students. The struggle between NYSUT and charter advocates then and now is about the character of a public good and, in turn, has served to more sharply mark the contested terrain of public education (NYSUT, 2010c).

The high-stakes battle played out in the New York state legislature was triggered by federal Race to the Top legislation, which rewarded states for developing charter schools. This point was confirmed by *The New York Times* when it remarked that the state senate's decision to lift the cap, "would more than double the number of charter schools, a move seen as key to helping the state win up to 700 million in federal grant money" (Medina, 2010a). NYSUT's vigorous lobbying yielded a number of concessions regarding the responsibilities of charters to a larger public. Their initially more ambitious New York State Charter School Act advanced the following agenda:

- *Transparency and accountability on fiscal data.* More to the point, this item was intended to bring charters into compliance with a recent Court of Appeals decision, which allows both financial and operational audits by New York state and New York City comptrollers. It was also proposed that the data be made public under the Freedom of Information Law.

- *Ethics reform for operators and board members of charter schools.* The goal was to subject charters to the same financial disclosure and conflict of interest prohibitions that their public counterparts are subject to. Equally important, a ban was sought on for-profit operators owning or operating a charter and disclosure of charter salaries. Finally, it was declared that school employees should be protected from anti-union animus.

- *Equity.* The intent is for charters to serve the district-wide average of neediest students, including English language learners and special education students. Equally important, it was felt that the charter lottery needed oversight and monitoring by a third party to ensure fairness of decision making and access. Finally, it was proposed that charter effectiveness records needed to document out-migration and reasons for this exit flow of students.

- *Geographic distribution and resultant oversaturation of charters in particular areas.* As a target of reform, this is a particularly critical issue given the stated tactical intention of charter advocates to saturate selected areas to supplant public education. The debilitating impact of such practices on public schools was noted. In addition, this provision would have required a remedy to the stress associated with co-location of public and charter schools at a single site.

- *Fair funding.* This issue is framed as a particularly acute problem for public schools, as the rapid expansion of charters was fueled in part by the neglect of public school financing. It was on this basis that NYSUT indicated that "charter school funding cannot come at the expense of public-school funding."

A number of critical issues were not raised by NYSUT in its legislative proposal. To begin with, equity in funding for charters with their counterparts is often raised by advocates as necessary to level the playing field. This of course makes sense if charters are also carrying the same public obligations or responsibilities as public systems. But as Gary Miron has recently noted:

Traditional public schools have additional obligations, accounting for much or all those funding differences. On first appearance, charter schools receive less revenue ($9,883) than traditional public schools. Yet this comparison they add may be misleading. While public schools receive revenues and money for such services as special education, student support services, transportation and food service, charter schools with few exceptions spend far less on these services which largely explain[s] the differences in revenue and expenditure. . . . Compared with traditional public schools, charters schools spend proportionately more on administration—in the percentage of overall spending that goes to administrative costs, as well as salaries they pay administrative personnel. Overall, however, charter schools spend less than traditional schools: less on instruction, less on student support services and less on teacher salaries and benefits. (Miron & Urshel, 2010, pp. 1–2).

Equally important, the NYSUT proposal did not raise critical issues of charter accountability to the communities where they are situated. Indeed, a state legislator in New Jersey is proposing that any charter application must be approved by the citizens of the community in which that charter would be located. This proposal is responsive to the problem that charter boards are often removed from local communities and that the regional and national character of many charter networks often distances them from the specific local concerns of communities and parents.

What then did NYSUT win in its fight to make charters more accountable and thus more public? The bill that was ultimately passed bars the opening of any for-profit charter schools, asserts that parents have a say in the co-location of charters and public schools, and insists that students "who are still learning English[,] have disabilities[,] or receive free or reduced price lunches be enrolled with comparable numbers to their local school districts." Clearly, much work remains in remaking charters into public institutions with the same funding and obligations as traditional schools. Until this occurs, present charter policies ensuring rapid expansion and exemption will be responsible for creating two separate and highly unequal systems of public education, one relatively starved, with a range of accountability demands, the other effectively private and relatively free of a collective accountability but with substantial access to government resources. It is within this contested terrain of restructuring public institutions that the present battle for public education is largely being waged.

## REIMAGINING AND REINVESTING IN A PUBLIC EDUCATION

We have been very clear throughout this volume about the potential value of limited experiments with charter schooling. Programs like the Harlem Children's Zone (HCZ) in New York City and North Star in Newark are making a discernable difference with a segment of urban students who remain in their schools. These experiments, however, depend on substantial private investment, and questions about impact, retention of students, and faculty continue to circulate. While we have great respect for the visions and leaders of both institutions, it's important to be honest about the impact and conditions under which they operate. Estimates are that HCZ's budget is two-thirds private investment and one-third public. Further, the sustainability and generalizability of these experiments are precarious. That said, national policies should not be shaped by exemplar experience.

This promises to be a period of significant political and policy fallout. The Tea Party offers but a first sip from the red-hot electoral-political kettle no longer able to contain the steam of economic decline. In this moment of tumult, reengineering public institutions into more privatized and deregulated forms remains the simple, cost-free political solution to downsizing and fixing the state. Exploiting the pain and historic neglect of low-income communities of color to advocate for privatization as a matter of national policy is especially perverse in this historic moment of economic crisis. But as we have argued throughout this book—and evidence from the subprime mortgage fallout, higher education rates of defaulting on loans, and charter reform suggest—such policy initiative is both expansive and ultimately undermining to the poorest communities of color. Community pushback against this trend in major urban areas is growing.

Therefore, it seems obvious that a large part of the impetus to improve public schools has and will continue to come from grassroots coalitions of parents, community members, educators, and youth. For example, five years ago grassroots groups in New York City successfully resisted the transfer of public schools to the for-profit Edison Project. Market competition and profit making were seen as eroding, not supporting, their goals for heightened classroom investment, community inclusion in decision making, and the efficient use of public dollars. At the time this fight led by ACORN was the cutting edge of a grassroots pushback against profit-making market alternatives to public education. With similar commitments, as noted in Chapter 5, in 2010, parents, youth, and educators successfully blocked school closings throughout New York City concerned, in part, that new schools would be opened as charters and, thus, inaccessible to local youth. In 2011, thousands of parents, students, and educators joined to denounce the mayor's and chancellor's decision to close another round of schools.

In January 2011, the Annenberg Institute for School Reform published a significant volume on the demonstrated impact of community organizing as a key element of education reform, "The Strengths and Challenges of Community Organizing as an Education Reform Strategy" (Renee & McAlister, 2011). Perhaps in response to NCLB and Race to the Top, across the nation we see an expanding number of organizing initiatives dedicated to educational justice emerging from a cross-section of communities. Their platforms cohere around resisting school closings, fighting for local strategic investment in traditional public education, and, most generally, struggling against the erosion of local school accountability.

In related campaigns, educators are mobilizing with parents and youth for alternatives to high-stakes testing; equal access to well resourced schools; college preparatory education; credentialed educators; and exposure to arts, music, and ethnic studies. (See the Grassroots Education Movement in New York City, grassrootseducationmovement.blogspot. com; New York Collective of Radical Educators [NYCORE], www.nycore. org; the Center for Immigrant Families; Class Size Matters, www.class sizematters.com; Urban Youth Collaborative, www.urbanyouthcollabora-tive.org; Caucus for Rank and File Educators in Chicago; Padres y Jóvenes Unidos in Denver, www.padresunidos.org; Inner City Struggle and Community Coalition in Los Angeles; the Annenberg Institute for School Reform; the Coalition for Educational Justice in New York City, www.nyccej. com; the Educational Justice Collaborative in Los Angeles, idea.gseis.ucla. edu/about/.../educational-justice-collaborative-ejc; and Southern Echo in Mississippi, www. Southernecho.org. See Rethinking Schools for analyses of these movements, www.rethinkingschools.com.)

Grassroots parent and teacher groups are beginning to broaden their base by reaching out to civil rights, religious, youth, and labor groups. These broad multiconstituency coalitions are best able to effectively infuse into the education reform dialogue old-fashioned values like democracy, racial justice, and community, providing the best hope of producing a strong progressive counterforce in the war for public schooling.

In the contested terrain of public education, logic and empirical record matter little. What matters most is power. The right wing, with "democratic" allies, has developed the power necessary to ever more deeply etch its imprint on public education. Any change in agenda will require the creation of new political formations organizing an army of parents and students to aggressively challenge the public discourse.

We can offer no single blueprint for the creation of new alignments of power or a reform platform that resonates with the larger electorate. To create such a blueprint would be both dishonest and foolish. We can, however, identify touchstones essential to the development of this critical political work. They include, but are not limited to, the following items:

- To advance a progressive agenda for public education reform, matters of historic inequality, and persistent structural racism, economic justice and equity of investment will need to be integrated into movements for a democratic, equitable, and accountable public education system.
- Progressive coalitions of educators, parents, youth, and community must win back the identity of critic, reformer, and innovator. Presently, the Right has a monopoly on this language and identity. If the Left is to be perceived as an agent of progressive change, then we must have a proactive agenda/platform that matches such aspiration and takes on critical conversations about the capitalization of public education dollars, educational quality, testing, equitable access to skilled and culturally engaged educators, deep accountability, class size, school "choice," selective admissions, discipline, critical pedagogy, and schools' relations with local communities.
- Finance equity and racial justice must be a foundational lens on our framework for change. There must be a clear message that restores faith in the belief that strategic public investment in education, enacted through equity, lies at the heart of democracy. While money can undoubtedly be spent poorly, the absence of resources dooms school systems and communities to decay.

- Democratic frameworks for accountability must be developed with a wide array of indicators, for example, in relationship to critical thinking, writing skills, and civic engagement by participatory coalitions of educators, parents, communities, and youth so that we can authentically hold state legislators and school districts accountable to deliver an inquiring education combined with a more critical performance-based palette of standards. It is time to expose and challenge the dangers of public policies that exclusively rely upon standardized testing for evaluating students, teachers, school report cards, school closings, and charter development. And we must attack the rigidity of bureaucracy that has resisted the influence of community and educators.
- Organizing, mobilization, and advocacy must be at the center of any political work developed by progressive organizations. The legislature and other branches of government will not listen unless the numbers of progressive activists swell dramatically. That can only happen with effective organizing campaigns. We can't outspend our adversaries or have greater access to the media. What we can do is out-organize them. Organizational investments of time and dollars need to comport with this reality. If the neoliberal attack on public education has had any "good outcome," it is the renewed and reenergized organizing of educators, parents, communities, and youth for educational justice.
- Teacher unions must change. Unions' practice must evolve more robust forms of social unionism, which produce an enlarged sense of community extending beyond members to the communities they serve. This work requires teachers and their unions to struggle to understand community perspective on schooling issues. To alter that dynamic, teacher unions must spend a good deal of time reaching out to, and building relationships of alliance with, parents, youth, and educators on the ground and with community-based advocates, working on peer review and democratic accountability that would include community groups in thinking through what constitutes good teaching and school-community relations.

Clearly, this contestation over the future direction of public education will be waged over the long term. New formations will not change the present discourse or balance of power in the short run. However, the work now is to begin creating new alliances, platforms for change and organizing campaigns in targeted cities. This is a struggle for public education, the fabric of a multiracial democracy and economic justice.

## CONCLUSION

We are effectively at a crossroads as a nation. Structural inequality gaps etched in class and race formations are widening and must be redressed through multipronged coalitions focused on a politics of redistribution and solidarity across public institutions, including traditional schools, public charters, and public higher education. Indeed, democracy depends upon a durable set of public institutions and relationships that build diverse communities over time and generations—libraries, highways, sanitation services, police, parks, hospitals, subways/buses, EMTs, environmental protections, youth-building organizations, and schools. These are the sites where we come face-to-face with our shared fates; these are the sites where democracy and equity are under siege.

Entering the contested terrain of public education is an essential act of citizenship precisely because it demonstrates our commitment to preserving a racially and economically just public sphere and larger democracy. Either we are prepared to struggle for a future built on a rock-solid foundation of a well-funded education system available for all children, or we all suffer in the quicksand of shifting resources from a starved public education system to privatized alternatives. Nothing less than the very future of public schooling and a larger democratic culture and politics is at stake.

# References

American Federation of Teachers. (2009). *State revenue systems: Options for the current crisis.* Washington DC: American Federation of Teachers.

Anand, B., Fine, M., Perkins, T., & Surrey, D., with Kinoy, A. (2002). *Keeping the struggle alive.* New York: Teachers College Press.

Anderson, N. (2010, January 30). Education Secretary Duncan calls Hurricane Katrina good for New Orleans schools. *Washington Post,* p. 1. http://www.washingtonpost.com/wp-dyn/content/article/2010/01/29/AR2010012903259.html (retrieved June 15, 2010)

Anyon, J. (1997). *Ghetto schooling.* New York: Teachers College Press.

Ayers, W., & Tanner, R. A. (2010). *To teach: The journey in comics.* New York: Teachers College Press.

Baker, B. (2010, January). More fun with New Jersey charters. Retrieved February 15, 2011, from http://schoolfinance101.wordpress.com/2010/01/26/more-fun-with-new-jersey-charter-schools/

Barkan, Joanne. (2011, Winter). Got dough? How billionaires rule our schools. *Dissent Magazine.* Retrieved September 8, 2011, from http://www.dissentmagazine.org/article/?article=3781

Barr, J. M., Sadovnik, A. R., & Visconti, L. (2006). Charter schools and urban education improvement: A comparison of Newark's district and charter schools. *Urban Review, 36*(4), 291–312.

Bell, D. (1993). *Faces at the bottom of the well.* New York: Basic Books.

Bennett, J. (2010, May 27). Vanishing students, rising scores: Middle school charters show alarming student attrition over time. Retrieved June 10, 2010, from http://www.edwize.org

Bettinger, E. P. (2005, April). The effect of charter schools on charter students and public schools. *Economics of Education Review, 24*(2), 133–147.

Bloomfield, D. C. (2009). Small schools: Myth and reality. In *NYC schools under Bloomberg and Klein: What parents, teachers, and policymakers need to know* (pp. 49–56). New York: Lulu.

Booker, T. K., Sass, T., Gill, B., & Zimmer, R. (2010, Spring). The unknown world of charter high schools. *Education Next, 10,* 70–75.

Bowles, S., & Gintis, H. (1977). *Schooling in capitalist America.* New York: Basic Books.

Bracey, G. (2004, March). *City-wide systems of charter schools: Proceed with caution.* Tempe, AZ: Education Policies Studies Laboratory, Education Policy Research Unit, Arizona State University.

Bracey, G. (2005, May). *Charter schools: Performance and accountability—a disconnect.* Tempe, AZ: Education Policies Studies Laboratory, Education Policy Research Unit, Arizona State University.

Brandon, A., & Weiher, G. R. (2007, April 12). The impact of competition: Charter schools and public schools in Texas. Paper presented at Midwestern Political Science Association, Chicago, IL.

Braun, B. (2010, September 27). Idea of failing public schools promoted by politicians, privatizers and celebrities. Retrieved July 21, 2011, from http://blog.nj.com/njv_bob_braun/2010/09/bob_braun_idea_of_failing_nj_p.html

Bridgeland, J., DiIulio, J., & Morison, K. (2006, March). *The silent epidemic: Perspectives of high school dropouts.* Seattle, WA: Bill and Melinda Gates Foundation.

Brooks, D. (2009, October 23). The quiet revolution. *The New York Times*, p. A35.

Brown, P. M. (2006). Municipally operated charter schools: A new trend in community services. *Education and Urban Society, 39*(3), 3–18.

Buckley, J., & Sattin-Bajaj, C. (2010). *Are ELL students underrepresented in charter schools?* (Report NYC 2006–2008). New York, NY: National Center for the Study of Privatization in Education.

Cappelaro, C. (2005, Summer). Interview with Hector Calderon: When small is beautiful: Bargaining for better schools. *Rethinking Schools.* Retrieved September 6, 2011, from http://www.rethinkingschools.org/special_reports/quality_teachers/beau194.shtml

Cardinale, Matthew. (2009, November 28). Education-US: Social justice schools shape new wave of activists. Retrieved from http://www.globalissues.org/news/2009/11/28/3693

Center for Community Change. (2008). *Dismantling a community.* Washington, DC: Center for Community Change.

Center for Education Reform. (2009, March 9). Accountability lies at the heart of charter school success. Retrieved September 8, 2011, from http://www.edreform.com/Vital_Links/Charter_School_Achievement/?Accountability_Lies_at_the_Heart_of_Charter_School_Success

Center for Research on Education Outcomes (CREDO). (2009). *Multiple choice: Charter school performance in 16 states.* Stanford, CA: Stanford University.

Chicago Public Schools. (n.d.). Office of new schools. Retrieved January 9, 2010, from http://www.cps.edu/NEWSCHOOLS/Pages/ONS.aspx

Clarke, M., Haney, W., & Madaus, G. (2000). High stakes testing and high school completion. National Board on Educational Testing and Public Policy, Boston College. Retrieved July 11, 2011, from http://www.bc.edu/research/nbetpp/publications/v1n3.html

Committee on Education and the Workforce. (2009). Retrieved March 4, 2010, from http://democrats.edworkforce.house.gov/newsroom/2009/05/high-school-dropout-crisis-thr.shtml

Communities for Excellent Public Schools. (2010a). *A proposal for sustainable school transformation.* Retrieved July 11, 2011, from http://www.ceps-ourschools.org/pdfs/Sustainable_School_Transformation_Proposal_English.pdf

Communities for Excellent Public Schools. (2010b). *Our communities left behind: An analysis of the administration's school turnaround policies.* Retrieved from www.

ceps-ourschools.org

Cook, A., & Tashlik, P. (2005). Standardizing small. *Rethinking Schools, 20*(3), 60–63.

Cramer, P. (2009, March 26). *Public advocate hopeful takes aim at DOE's spending on testing.* Retrieved July 11, 2011, from http://gothamschools.org/2009/03/26/public-advocate-hopeful-takes-aim-at-does-spending-on-testing/

Darling-Hammond, L. (2009). President Obama and education: The possibility for dramatic improvements in teaching and learning. *Harvard Educational Review, 79*(2), 210–223.

Darling-Hammond, L. (2010a). *The flat world and education: How America's commitment to equity will determine our future.* New York: Teachers College Press.

Darling-Hammond, L. (2010b, October) School improvement. *NJEA Review,* 13–14.

de la Torre, M., & Gwynne, J. (2009). *When schools close: Effects on displaced students in Chicago public schools.* Consortium on Chicago School Research. Retrieved February 14, 2010, from http://ccsr.uchicago.edu/content/publications.php?pub_id=136

Delpit, L. (2006). *Other people's children.* New York: New Press.

Democrats for Education Reform. (2008). *Flooding the zone: How an intense, focused school choice campaign in Harlem increased support for reform.* Democrats for Education Reform, New York, NY.

Dietz, S. (2010, December 21). *State high school tests: Exit exams and other assessments.* Washington, DC: Center on Education Policy.

Dillon, S. (2009, June 22). Education chief to warn advocates that inferior charter schools harm the effort. *New York Times,* p. A10.

Dingerson, L., Miner, B., Peterson, B., Walters, S. (Eds.). (2008). *Keeping the promise? The debate over charter schools.* Milwaukee, WI: Rethinking Schools.

Dingerson, L. (2008). *Reclaiming the education charter: Ohio's experiment with charter schooling.* Washington, DC: Education Voters Institute, The Forum for Democracy and Change.

Dixon, B. A. (2009, July 1). Obama's public education policy: Privatization, charters, mass firings, neighborhood, and family destabilization. Black Agenda Report. Retrieved July 25, 2011, from http://www.blackagendareport.com/content/obamas-public-education-policy-privatization-charters-mass-firings-neighborhood-destabilizat

Dobbie, W., & Fryer, R. G., Jr. (2009). *Are high-quality schools enough to close the achievement gap? Evidence from a bold social experiment in Harlem.* Cambridge, MA: Harvard University.

Du Bois, W. E. B. (1910). *The crisis magazine.* Retrieved from http://www.thecrisismagazine.com

Du Bois, W. E. B. (1970). The freedom to learn. In P. S. Foner (Ed.), *W. E. B. Du Bois speaks* (pp. 230–231). New York: Pathfinder.

El-Amine, Z., & Glazer, L. (2008). Evolution or destruction?: The case of Washington D.C. In L. Dingerson, B. Miner, R. Peterson, & S. Walters (Eds.), *Keeping the promise: The debate over charter schools.* Milwaukee, WI: Rethinking Schools.

Esparza, S. (2009, December 13). Detroit parents want DPS teachers, officials jailed over low test scores. *Detroit News.* Retrieved from http://detnews.com

Fabricant, M. (2010). *Organizing for educational justice: The campaign for public school reform in the South Bronx.* Minneapolis: University of Minnesota Press.

Fabricant, M. (2011a). Organizing for equity. *American Educator, 35*(1), 36–40.

Fabricant, M. (2011b). Reimagining labor: The lessons of Wisconsin. *Working USA: The Journal of Labor and Society, 15*(1).

Fabricant, M., & Fisher, R. (2002). *Settlement houses under siege: The struggle to sustain community organizations in New York City.* New York: Columbia University Press.

Farrie, D., & Fine, M. (2010). *Report card on secondary charters in New Jersey: An analysis of charter high schools' equity in access, student achievement, cohort persistence and graduation pathways.* Unpublished manuscript, Newark, New Jersey: Education Law Center and the CUNY Graduate Center.

Finch, H., Lapsey, D., & Baker-Boudissa, M. (2009). A survival analysis of student mobility and retention in Indiana charter schools. *Education Policy Analysis Archives, 17*(8), 1–14.

Fine, M. (1991). *Framing dropouts.* Albany: SUNY Press.

Fine, M. (2005). Not in our name. *Rethinking Schools, 19*(4), 11–14.

Fine, M., Pappas, L., Karp, S., Hirsch, L., Sadovnik, A., Keeton, A., et al. (2009). *New Jersey's Special Review Assessment: Loophole or lifeline?* Newark, NJ: Education Law Center, Institute for Education Law and Policy, Project GRAD and the Graduate Center of the City University of New York. Retrieved March 3, 2010, from http://ielp.rutgers.edu/docs/SRA_Policy_Brief_final.pdf

Fine, M., & Ruglis, J. (2008). Circuits of dispossession: The racialized and classed realignment of the public sphere for youth in the U.S. *Transforming Anthropology, 17*(1) 20–33.

Foote, M. (2007). Keeping accountability systems accountable. *Phi Delta Kappan, 88*(05), 359–363.

Fox, M., Mediratta, K., Stoudt, B., Ruglis, J., Fine, M., & Salah, S. (2010). Critical youth engagement: Participatory action research and organizing. In L. Sherrod, J. Torney-Purta, & C. Flanagan, *Handbook of research on civic engagement in youth* (pp. 621 – 650). Hoboken, NJ: John Wiley.

Frankenberg, E., & Lee, C. (2003*). Charter schools and race: A lost opportunity for integrated education.* Cambridge, MA: Harvard University, The Civil Rights Project. Retrieved from http://www.civilrightsproject. harvard.edu/research/deseg/Charter_Schools03.pdf

Fruchter, N. (2007) *Urban schools, public will.* New York: Teachers College Press.

Gabriel, T., & Medina, J. (2010, May 9). Charters schools' new cheerleaders: Financiers. *New York Times.* Retrieved November 14, 2010, from http://www.nytimes.com/2010/05/10/nyregion/10charter.html

Garcia, D. R. (2008). Academic and racial segregation in charter schools: Do parents sort students into specialized charter schools? *Education and Urban Society, 40*(5), 590–612.

Glass, G. V. (2008). *Fertilizers, pills, and magnetic strips: The fate of public education in America.* Charlotte, NC: Information Age Publishing.

Gleason, P., Clark, M., Tuttle, C., & Dwoyer, E. (2010, June). *The evaluation of charter school impacts: Final report.* Washington, DC: U.S. Department of Education.

Golden, D. (2010, July 19–25). Teachers pest: The Bill and Melinda Gates Foundation betting billions that a business approach can work in the classroom. *Bloomberg Business Week*. Retrieved June 20, 2010, from http://www.businessweek.com/magazine/toc/10_30/B4188magazine.htm

Goldsmith, S. (2010, April 1). Uproar over "cozy" relationship between Chancellor Klein, charter school boss Eva Moskowitz. *New York Daily News*. Retrieved April 19, 2010, from http://articles.nydailynews.com/.../27060549_1_charter-school-public-schools-school-officials-show

Gonzalez, J. (2010, October 10). Local charter schools like Harlem Success are big business as millions are poured into marketing. Retrieved July 25, 2011, from http://articles.nydailynews.com/2010-10-01/local/27076850_1_charter-schools-local-charter-success-academy

Grossman, A., & Curran, D. (2004). *The Harlem Children's Zone: Driving performance with measurement and evaluation*. Boston, MA: Harvard Business School Publishing.

Grossman, K. (2005, September 5). $63 million worth it to Little Village. *Chicago Sun-Times*.

Hanushek, E., Kain, J., & Rivkin, S. (2002). The impact of charter schools on academic achievement. Retrieved from http://edpro.stanford.edu/eah/papers/charters.aea. jan03.pdf

Harris, D. C. (2007). Should I stay or should I go? Comparing teacher mobility in Florida's charter and tradition public schools. *Peabody Journal of Education, 82*(2/3), 274–310.

Harvey, D. (2004) A geographer's perspective on the new American imperialism. Conversations with history. Berkeley, CA: UC Institute of International Studies. Retrieved May 10, 2007 from http://globetrotter.berkeley.edu/people4/Harvey/harvey-con0.html

Hass, N. (2009, December 6). Scholarly investments: How charter schools became the hot cause for hedge fund managers. *New York Times*, Sunday Styles, p. 1.

Hedges, C. (2009). *Empire of illusion: The end of literacy and the triumph of spectacle*. New York: Nation Books.

Henig, J. R. (2008). *Spin cycle, how research is used in policy debates: The case of charter schools*. New York: Russell Sage Foundation.

Horn, J. (2010, April 27). Charter school news: Imagine charter schools seems to be more interested in profit and real estate as part of their charter business model. Retrieved from www.schoolsmatter.info/2010_03_01_archive.html

Hoxby, C. (2004). *A straightforward comparison of charter schools and regular public schools in the United States*. Unpublished manuscript. Cambridge, MA: Harvard University.

Hoxby, C. M., Murarka, S., & Kang, J. (2009, September). *How New York City's charter schools affect achievement, August 2009 report* (second report in series). Cambridge, MA: New York City Charter Schools Evaluation Project.

Hu, W. (2010, May 20). Teachers facing the weakest market for jobs in years: Battered by recession, applicants far outpace openings. *New York Times*, p. A1.

Institute on Race and Policy. (2008, November). *Failed promises: Assessing charter schools in the twin cities*. Minneapolis: University of Minnesota Law School.

Institute on Race and Poverty. (2010, May 15). *State of public schools in post-Katrina New Orleans: The challenge of creating equal opportunity*. Minneapolis, MN:

University of Minnesota Law School.

Jackson, C. (2010). Immigrant charter schools a better choice? *Education Digest,* *75*(9), 23–27.

Jennings, J. L., & Haimson, L. (2009). *High school discharges revisited: Trends in New York City's discharge rates, 2000–2007.* New York: Columbia University, Department of Sociology & Class Size Matters.

Jennings, J. L., & Pallas, A. M. (2010). *Do New York City's new small schools enroll students with different characteristics from other schools?* Providence, RI: Annenberg Institute.

Jensen, N., Kisida, B., McGee, J., & Ritter, G. (2010). A closer look at charter schools and segregation: Flawed comparisons lead to overstated conclusions. *Education Next, 10*(3). Retrieved July 25, 2011, from http://educationnext. org/a-closer-look-at-charter-schools-and-segregation/

Kahlenberg, R. (2008). The charter schools idea turns 20. *Education Week, 27*(29), 24.

Karp, S. (2006). Band-aids or bulldozers. *Rethinking Schools,* Spring. Retrieved from http://www.rethinkingschools.org/special_reports/bushplan/band203.shtml

Karp, S. (2010). Superhero school reform. *Rethinking Schools, 25*(2), 12–17. Retrieved from http://www.rethinkingschools.org/archive/25_02/25_02_karp.shtml

Klein, N. (2007). *The shock doctrine: The rise of disaster capitalism.* New York: Picador.

Kolodner, M. (2010, April 8; 2011, May 13). Charter schools on hook for thousands of dollars in interest payments to for-profit company. *Daily News.* Retrieved July 25, 2011, from http://www.nydailynews.com/ny_local/ education/2010/04/08/2010-04-08_charter_schools_lesson_in_finance.html

Kozol, J. (1972). *Free schools.* New York: Houghton Mifflin.

Krashen, S. (2010, October 14). *The problem is poverty.* Retrieved December 15, 2011, from http://www.schoolsmatter.info/2010/10/problem-is-poverty

Krugman, P. (2010, May 13). We're not Greece. *The New York Times.* Retrieved September 8, 2011, from http://www.nytimes.com/2010/05/14/ opinion/14krugman.html

Ladd, H., & Bifulco, R. (2004). *The impacts of charter schools on student achievement: Evidence from North Carolina* (Working Paper SAN04–01). Durham, NC: Terry Sanford Institute of Public Policy, Duke University.

Lawyers Committee for Civil Rights Under the Law et al. (2010, July). *Framework for providing all students an opportunity to learn through reauthorization of the elementary and secondary education act.* Retrieved July 25, 2011, from http:// naacpldf.org/files/case_issue/Framework%20for%20Providing%20All%20 Students%20an%20Opportunity%20to%20Learn%202.pdf

Lee, K. (2009). Do charter schools spur improved efficiency in traditional public schools in Michigan? *KEDI Journal of Educational Policy, 6*(1), 41–59.

Levin, H. M. (2001). *Privatizing education: Can the marketplace deliver choice, efficiency, equity, and social cohesion?* Cambridge. MA: Westview Press.

Lewis, K. (2010, June 12). CTU president-elect acceptance speech. Retrieved from http://coreteachers.com/2010/06/13/karen-lewis-ctu-president-elect- acceptance-speech/

Libby, K. (2010a). *Chartering possibilities—first in a series.* Retrieved from http:// www.schoolsmatter.info/2010/07/chartering-possibilities-first-in.html

Libby, K. (2010b). *Expanding to scale:* Part 11 of a series. Retrieved July 25, 2011 from http://www.schoolsmatter.info/2010/07/expanding-to-scale-part-ii-of-series_21.html

Lindquist, B. (2009, November 24). Growing pains: Scaling up the nation's best charter schools. *Education Sector Reports.* Retrieved December 14, 2009, from http://www.docstoc.com/docs/17640414/Growing-Pains-Scaling-Up-the-Nations-Best-Charter-Schools

Lipman, P. (2002). Making the global city, making inequality: The political economy and cultural politics of Chicago school policy. *American Education Research Journal, 39,* 379.

Lipman, P. (2011). *The new political economy of urban education: Neo-liberalism, race and the right to the city.* New York: Routledge.

Lipman, P., & Hursh, D. (2007). Renaissance 2010: The reassertion of ruling- class power through neoliberal policies in Chicago. *Policy Futures in Education, 5*(2), 160–178.

Mack, J. (2010, February 15). Charter schools split along racial lines; new study finds parents' choices accelerate resegregation. *Kalamazoo Gazette.* Retrieved July 25, 2011, from http://www.mlive.com/news/kalamazoo/index.ssf/2010/02/charter_schools_split_along_ra.html

Marshall, A. (2010, May 18). 10 northeast Ohio charter school boards sue White Hat management firm. Retrieved July 25, 2011, from http://www.cleveland.com/open/index.ssf/2010/05/for-profit_management_company.html

Master Charter School webpage (accessed July 2011). Speech by President Barack Obama, July 29, 2010. http://www.masterycharter.org/index.html

Maxwell, L. (2010, June 29). Study finds no clear edge for charters. *Education Week.* Retrieved from www.edweek.org/ew/articles/2010/06/29/36ies.h29.html

McGray, D. (2009, May 11). The instigator: A crusader's plan to remake failing schools. *New Yorker,* 66–74.

Medina, J. (2009a, November 30). City's schools share space and bitterness with charters. *New York Times,* p. A-1.

Medina, J. (2009b, April 29). Number of students leaving school early continues to increase, study says. *New York Times.* Retrieved November 7, 2009, from http://www.nytimes.com/2009/04/30/education/30graduation.html

Medina, J. (2009c, October 14). U.S. math tests find scant gains across New York. *New York Times.* Retrieved July 25, 2011, from http://www.nytimes.com/2009/10/15/education/15scores.html

Medina, J. (2010a, May 3). State senate approves bill to increase charter schools. *New York Times,* Retrieved http://www.nytimes.com/2010/05/04/nyregion

Medina, J. (2010b, May 7). In Harlem, epicenter for charter schools, a senator wars against them. *New York Times,* p. A22.

Meier, D. (2002). *The power of their ideas.* Cambridge: Beacon Press.

Meier, D. (2005). Creating democratic schools. *Rethinking Schools, 19*(4), 28–29.

Mickelson, R., Bottia, M., & Southworth, S. (2008). School choice and segregation by race, class, and achievement. Retrieved from http://epsl.asu.edu/epru/

documents/EPSL-0803-260-EPRU.pdf

Miron, G., & Dingerson, L. (2009, October 7). Time to get off the expansion expression: Is proliferation of the charter school market interfering with its quality? *Education Week*, p. D-42.

Miron, G., & Urschel, J. (2009). *Profiles of nonprofit education management organizations: 2008*. Department of Educational Leadership, Western Michigan University, Kalamazoo, MI.

Miron, G., & Urshel, J. (2010, June). *Equal or fair? A study of revenues and expenditures in American charter schools*. East Lansing: MI: The Great Lakes Center for Education Research and Practice.

Molnar, A. (1996a). *Giving kids the business: The commercialization of America's schools*. Boulder, CO: Westview Press.

Molnar, A. (1996b, October). Charter school: The smiling face of disinvestment. *Educational Leadership, 54*(2), 1–7.

Molnar, A. (2005) *School commercialism: From democratic ideal to market commodity*. Routledge: New York.

Molnar, A., Garcia, D., Miron, G., & Berry, S. (2007). *Profiles of for profit education management organizations*. Education Policies Studies Laboratory, Tempe, AZ.

Monahan, R. (2008, November 13). Teaching for the test doesn't mean learning, UFT pres says: Test prep fever equals math dummies. *New York Daily News*. Retrieved July 25, 2011, from http://articles.nydailynews.com/2009-11-13/local/17938779_1_testing-obsession-college-math-middle-school-math

Monahan, R. (2010, March 28). Manhattan Supreme Court saved 19 schools, education department plays musical chairs with new schools. *New York Daily News*. Retrieved May 11, 2010, from http://www.nydailynews.com/ny_local/education/2010/03/28/2010-03-28_19_schools_are_saved_now_others_play_musical_chairs.html#ixzz1BEORUrYG

Morris, J. E. (2009). *Troubling the waters: Fulfilling the promise of quality public schooling for Black children*. New York: Teachers College Press.

Moses, R., & Cobb, C. (2002). *Radical equations*. Boston, MA: Beacon Press.

Mulgrew, M. (2010, April 17). *Remapping progressive education*. Presented at the Deborah Meier Symposium, New York.

*Mulgrew v. Board of Education*. (2010). Available at http://www.courts.state.ny.us/Reporter/3dseries/2011/2011_21030.htm

National Council of Churches Governing Board. (2010, May 19). Pastoral letter to the department of education. Available at http://www.nccusa.org/elmc/pastoralletter.PDF

New Jersey Department of Education. (2010). *Fall surveys enrollment*. Trenton, NJ.

New KIPP study underestimates attrition effects. (2010, September 27). Retrieved July 25, 2011, from http://nepc.colorado.edu/newsletter/2010/06/new-kipp-study-underestimates-attrition-effects-0

Ni, Y. (2009). The impact of charter schools on the efficiency of traditional public schools: Evidence from Michigan. *Economics of Education Review, 28*(5), 571–584.

New York State United Teachers (NYSUT). (2010a). *Following the money: Who funds the charter industry?* Author.

New York State United Teachers (NYSUT). (2010b). *Major findings: How right wing money and lack of oversight tilt the landscape in favor of charter schools*.

Author.

New York State United Teachers (NYSUT). (2010c). *The two billion dollar decision: The case for reforming New York's charter school law.* Author.

O'Donnell, D. (2009, February 26). [Letter to J. I. Klein]. Available at http://www.tilsonfunds.com/Personal/KeepingthePromiseWhitePapers.pdf

Orfield, G. (2001). *Schools more separate: Consequences of a decade of resegregation.* Cambridge, MA: Civil Rights Project, Harvard University.

Orfield, G. (2010, March 3). *Choice without equity: Charter school segregation and the need for civil rights standards.* Civil Rights Project/Proyecto Derechos Civiles at University of California, Los Angeles.

Otterman, S. (2010, October 12). Lauded Harlem Schools have own problems. *New York Times.* Retrieved from http://www.nytimes.com/2010/10/13/education/13harlem.html

Placencia, P. (2010, May). *Parent organizing and charters.* Medgar Evers College Forum on Ethnicity and School Organizing

Payne, C., & Strickland, C. (Eds.) (2008). *Teach freedom: Education for liberation in the African-American tradition.* New York: Teachers College Press.

Payne, C. M., & Knowles, T. (2009). Charter schools, urban school reform, and the Obama administration. *Harvard Educational Review, 79*(2), 227–239.

Petrilli, M. (2010, April 15). Teacher accountability: The next front in the school reform wars. *Education Next, 2.*

*Phi Delta Kappan.* (October 2010). 42nd Annual PDK/Gallup Poll. Retrieved July 25, 2011.from http://www.pdkintl.org/kappan/poll.htm

Powell, J., & Frankenberg, E. (2010, April 2). Charter schools and segregation. *Detroit Free Press.* Retrieved from http://www.freep.com/apps/pbcs.dll/article?AID=/20100402/OPINION05/100401083/1322/Charter-schools-and-segregation&template=fullarticle

Ravitch, D. (2009a). Introduction. In *NYC Schools under Bloomberg and Klein: What parents, teachers, and policymakers need to know* (pp. 1–22). New York: Lulu.

Ravitch, D. (2009b). Student achievement in New York City: The NAEP results. In *NYC Schools under Bloomberg and Klein: What parents, teachers, and policymakers need to know* (pp. 22–29). New York: Lulu.

Ravitch, D. (2010a). *The death and life of the great American school system: How testing and choice are undermining education.* New York: Basic Books.

Ravitch, D. (2010b, August 1). The sound of bubbles bursting: Student gains on state test vanished into thin air. *Daily News.* Retrieved July 25, 2011, from http://articles.nydailynews.com/2010-08-01/news/29438770_1_charter-students-student-gains-national-tests

Ravitch, D. (2010c, March 5). Interview with *Democracy Now.* Retrieved September 8, 2011, from http://www.democracynow.org/2010/3/5/protests

Reardon, S. F. (2009a). *Review of how New York City's charter schools affect achievement. Boulder and Tempe: Education and the Public Interest Center & Education Policy Research Unit.* Retrieved from http://epicpolicy.org/ thinktank/revew-How-New-York-City-Charter

Reardon, S. (2009b, November 12). *Headline grabbing charter school study doesn't hold up to scrutiny.* Boulder: Education and the Public Interest, School of

Education, University of Colorado at Boulder.

Reich, R. (2010, July 19/26). Inequality in America and what to do about it. *The Nation*, 15–17.

Renee, M., & McAlister, S. (2011). The strengths and challenges of community organizing as an education reform strategy. Providence, RI: Annenberg Institute for School Reform at Brown University. Retrieved November 10, 2011, from http://www.nmefdn.org/uploads/AISRCommunityOrganizingExecSum2011.pdf

Renzulli, L., & Evans, L. (2003). School choice, whose choice? Paper presented at the annual meeting of the American Sociological Association, Atlanta, GA. Retrieved from http://www.allacademic.com/ meta/p107679_index.html

Robelen, E. W. (2008). KIPP study finds high school attrition amid big learning gains. *Education Week, 28*(5), 10.

Rogosa, D. (2002). A further examination of student progress in charter schools using the California API. CRESST. Retrieved July 25, 2011, from http://www.cse.ucla.edu/products/reports/TR521.pdf

Roy, J., & Mishel, L. (2005). *Advantage none: Re-examining Hoxby's finding of charter school benefits* (Briefing Paper 158). Washington, DC: Economic Policy Institute. Retrieved from http://www.epinet.org/ content.cfm/bp

Ruglis, J., & Freudenberg, N. (2010). Toward a healthy high schools movement: Strategies for mobilizing public health for educational reform. *American Journal of Public Health, 100*(9), 1565–1571.

Schemo, D. (2004, August 16). Charter schools trail in results, U.S. data reveals. *New York Times*, p. A1.

Slovacek, S. P., Kunnan, A. J., & Kim, H. (3/11/2002). *California charter schools serving low SES students: An analysis of the academic performance index* (ERIC Document Reproduction Services No. 469 276). Retrieved July 15, 2011, from http://www.calstatela.edu/academic/ccoe/c_perc/rpt1.pdf

Spoto, M. A. (2010, March 18). NJ Gov Chris Christie leaves charter school budget untouched. Retrieved July 25, 2011, from http://www.nj.com/news/index.ssf/2010/03/gov_chris_christie_budget_leav.html

*Star Ledger* Staff. (2010, September 23). Oprah to host New Jersey Governor Christie, Newark Mayor Booker for $100M school gift by Facebook CEO. Retrieved July 25, 2011, from http://www.nj.com/news/index.ssf/2010/09/oprah_winfrey_nj_gov_chris_chr.html

Stoudt, B., Fox, M., & Fine, M. (n.d.). *The racialized patterns of stop and frisk practices in New York City: An analysis of growing up policed for adolescents of color and LGBT youth.* Unpublished manuscript. [To obtain a pdf, email bstoudt@jjay.cuny.edu]

Strauss, V. (2009, November 25). Why so many people are so angry at Arne Duncan. *Washington Post*. Retrieved July 25, 2011, from http://voices.washingtonpost.com/answer-sheet/no-child-left-behind/why-so-many-people-are-so-angr.html

Stuit, D., & Smith, T. (2009). *Teacher turnover in charter schools.* New York: National Center for the Study of Privatization in Education.

Toch, T. (2009a). *Charter management organizations: Expansion, survival and impact.* Retrieved from http://www.independenteducation.org/File%20Library/ Unassigned/Toch-Charter%20Management%20Organizations.pdf

Toch, T. (2009b). *Sweating the big stuff: A progress report on the movement to scale up the nation's best charter schools.* Unpublished manuscript.

Toppo, G. (2010, August 17). Objectives of charter schools with Turkish ties questioned. *USA Today.* Retrieved July 25, 2011, from http://www.usatoday.com/ news/education/2010-08-17-turkishfinal17_CV_N.htm

Tuttle, C., Nichols-Barrer, B. I., Gill, B., Gleason, P. (2010, June). *Student characteristics and achievement in 22 KIPP middle schools final report.* Washington, DC: Mathematica Policy Research.

United Federation of Teachers. (2010). *Victory management company background.* Author.

Valenzuela, A. (2004). *Leaving children behind: How Texas style accountability fails Latino youth.* Albany, NY: State University of New York Press.

Van Lier, P. (2010, May). *Public goods vs. private profit: imagine Schools, Inc. in Ohio.* Cleveland, OH: Policy Matters Ohio.

Viadero, D. (2009, December 22). Study casts doubt on strength of charter managers. *Education Week, 29*(14), 1, 13.

Walker, V. S. (1996). *Their highest potential: An African American school community in the segregated South.* Chapel Hill: University of North Carolina Press.

Wells, A. S. (2008). The social context of charter schools: The changing nature of poverty and what it means for American education. In M. G. Springer, H. J. Walberg, M. Berends, & D. Ballou (Eds.), *Handbook of research on school choice.* Philadelphia, PA: Lawrence Erlbaum.

Wells, A., & Roda, A. (2009) *White parents, diversity and school choice policies: Where good intentions, anxiety and privilege collide.* Peabody College, Vanderbilt University: National Center on School Choice.

Wilkinson, R., & Pickett, K. (2009). *The spirit level: Why greater equality makes societies stronger.* London: Bloomsbury Press.

Wolff, D. (2009, September 25). *The charter school gamble: Speculating on education.* Unpublished manuscript.

Woodson, C. (2010). *The miseducation of the Negro.* New York: Tribeca Books. (Original work published 1933)

Yun, J. (2010, March 25). *Private-public school report leaps to unsupported recommendations education and the public interest.* Boulder: School of Education, University of Colorado at Boulder.

Zelon, H. (2010, March). The charter challenge: The pros and conflicts of a schooling revolution. *City Limits, 34*(1), 17–21.

Zhao, Y. (2009). *Catching up or leading the way: American education in the age of globalization.* Alexandria, VA: ASCD.

Zimmer, R., & Buddin, R. (2009). Is charter school competition in California improving the performance of traditional public schools? *Public Administration Review, 69*(5), 831–845.

# Index

AARP, 64–65
Abbott schools (New Jersey), 121–122
Accountability
  of charter schools, 8, 25–26, 31, 35, 81, 83–84
  demands for, 81
  loss of, 84–86
  role of benefactors, 31
  testing in. *See* Testing
  transparency in, 123–124
Achievement First, 72
ACORN, 126
Admissions criteria, 7–8, 9
African Americans. *See also* "Crisis" of education
  equity and, 45–46
  tiers of schooling system, 33–34
Algiers Charter School District (Louisiana), 92–93
Allen, Jeanne, 94
Alliance for Excellent Education, 104–105
Alternative schools, 7
American Dream, 6
American Enterprise Institute, 65
American Federation of Teachers, 2, 84–85
Anand, B., 7, 88–89
Anderson, Nick, 91
Animo Leadership Charter School (Los Angeles), 15
Annenberg Institute for School Reform, 126–127
Anyon, J., 88
Arizona, 23–25, 71–72
Arroyo, Carmen, 74
Arroyo, Maria del Carmen, 74
Arroyo, Richard Izquierdo, 74
Aspire, 72
Assessment. *See* Testing
Authorization of charter schools, 23
Autonomy of charters, 24
Ayers, W., 88–89

Baker, Bruce, 38, 47–48, 55
Baker-Boudissa, Mary, 38, 49
Bakke, Dennis, 71
Baltimore, Maryland, 71
Barkan, Joanne, 64–66
Barr, J. M., 38, 39, 41
Barr, Steve, 15
Bell, D., 88
Benjamin Companies, 73–74
Bennett, J., 38
Berry, S., 32
Bettinger, Eric P., 38, 39, 42, 55
Bifulco, R., 38
Bill and Melinda Gates Foundation, 20, 29–30, 31, 63, 64–65, 104
Binary tradeoffs of charter policy, 109, 111–114
  competition/collaboration, 109, 112
  equitable/differential access, 109, 112–113
  exemplar performance/quality education for all, 109, 113
  reallocation/investment of resources, 109, 112
  simple/complex implementation of education reform agenda, 113–114
Bloomberg, Michael, 8, 42, 99
Bloomfield, David C., 100
Bond, Horace Mann, 104
Booker, T. K., 38
Bottia, M., 38
Bowles, S., 88
Bracey, G., 19, 25–26, 33, 42
Bradley, Harry, 67
Bradley, Lynde, 67
Bradley Foundation, 67
Brandon, A., 39, 55
Bridgeland, J., 104
Brighter Choice Foundation, 66–67, 76
Broader, Bolder Approach to Education, 118

Broad Foundation, 20, 29–30, 34–35, 64,
     65–66
Bronx Charter School for Children, 67
Bronx Charter School for Excellence, 67
Brooks, David, 12
Cheney, Dick, 67
Chicago
     innovation in, 53–54
     labor-community partnership in, 83
     Little Village/Lawndale High School,
          114, 115
     nonprofit charters in, 28
     Renaissance 2010 plan, 95–98, 102,
          105–107
     University of Chicago Charter Schools,
          16
China, 13
Choice ideology, 7, 20
Christie, Chris, 3, 84, 110
Civil rights, 3–4, 5–6, 38, 46, 118–119
Civil Rights Project, UCLA, 46
Clark, M., 38, 40
Clarke, Marguerite, 103
Class Size Matters, 127
Cleveland Academy of Math, Science and
     Technology (Ohio), 48
Clinton, Bill, 81
Coalition for Educational Justice (New York
     City), 127
Cobb, C., 88–89
Co-location, 8–9, 56–57
Colorado, 22, 24, 127
Comer, James, 52
Communities for Excellent Public Schools,
     38, 39
Connecticut, 71
Consortium on Chicago School Reform,
     96–98
Construction arrangements, 73–74, 75–76
Contract length, 24
Cook, A., 19, 24, 54, 88–89, 104–105
CORE (Caucus of Rank and File Educators),
     97–98, 127
Corruption, 30–31
     in assessment and accountability, 31
     educational management organizations
          (EMOs), 72–75
     fees for back-office support, 31
CREDO (Center for Research on Education
     Outcomes), 10, 25, 38–41, 43, 73

"Crisis" of education, 88–107
     Chicago Renaissance 2010 plan, 95–98,
          102, 105–107
     closings, 26, 72, 98–102
     "darker races" (Du Bois), 88–89
     dropout epidemic, 104–105
     landscape of inequality, 90–91
     New York City school closings/charter
          openings, 98–100, 101–102, 105–107
     in post-Katrina New Orleans, 91–95,
          105–106
     testing, 102–104
     tracking impact of dispossession,
          100–102
Cuomo, Andrew, 63
Curran, D., 38

Daley, Richard, 96
Darling-Hammond, Linda, 22, 38, 39, 57,
     103, 119–121
de la Torre, M., 38, 96, 97
Dell Foundation, 29
Delpit, L., 88
Democrats for Education Reform (DFER),
     3, 20, 48, 80–81
DiIulio, J., 104
Dillon, S., 41
Dingerson, Leigh, 17, 18–19, 21, 25, 32, 33,
     38, 39, 41, 43–45, 48, 50, 72–73
Diploma denial, 105–106
Dispossession. See "Crisis" of education
Dixon, B. A., 38
Dobbie, W., 38, 39
Dolores Huerta (Denver), 22
Doris and Donald Fisher Fund, 65
Dropout rates, 48–52, 101–102, 104–105
Du Bois, W. E. B., 5–6, 11, 33, 88, 89,
     99–100
Duncan, Arne, 7, 41, 63–65, 91
Dwoyer, E., 38, 40

Eberts, R., 42
Economic meltdown of 2008-2009, 12–14,
     77–78
Edison Schools, Inc., 21, 35–36, 58, 70–71,
     72, 126
Educational Alternatives, Inc., 71, 72
Educational Impact Statement (EIS), 99
Educational Justice Collaborative (Los
     Angeles), 127

Education Industry Association, 92
Education Law Center, 51
Education Management Organization
    (EMO), 23, 32–33, 66–75
Education Policy Studies Institute, 65
*Education Week*, 25
El-Amine, Zein, 49–50
Elementary and Secondary Education Act
    of 1965, 120
Eli and Edyth Broad Foundation, 20, 29–
    30, 34–35, 64, 65–66
English language learners (ELLs), 45–46,
    113
EPIC (Effective Practice Incentive
    Community), 16
Epstein, Joyce, 52
Equity
    adverse impact of inequality gaps,
        119–120
    English language learners (ELLs),
        45–46, 113
    immigrant students, 44–45, 127
    inequality and "crisis" of education,
        90–91
    poorest of the poor and, 47–48
    promise-evidence gap, 38, 45–48
    social stratification, 46–47, 90–91,
        94–95
    structural racism, 83
    students in special education, 45–46,
        113
Esparza, S., 34
*Evaluation of Charter School Impacts, The*
    (Gleason et al.), 40
Evans, L., 38, 47
Exemplar schools and networks, 14–17,
    109, 113
    exemplar schools, defined, 17
    Green Dot network (California), 15, 22,
        34 35, 72
    Harlem Children Zone (HCZ; New York
        City), 14–15, 29, 125–126
    KIPP (Knowledge is Power), 15–16, 22,
        49, 58–59, 72
    Uncommon Ground, 15–16
    University of Chicago Charter Schools,
        16

Fabricant, M., 36, 83, 89
Facebook, 30, 84

Fairtest, 84
Farrie, D., 38
Finch, Holmes, 38, 49
Fine, Michelle, 7, 24, 38, 48, 88–91,
    100–105
Finland, 121
Finn, Chester, 37–40
Fisher Foundation, 29
*Flat World and Education, The* (Darling-
    Hammond), 57
Folk Arts-Cultural Treasures Charter School
    (Philadelphia), 22, 114, 116–117
Foote, Martha, 84
Foundation for Education Reform and
    Accountability (FERA), 67
Foundations, 19–20, 29–30. *See also*
    Privatization *and names of specific*
    *foundations*
    influence of wealth on public policy, 63
    state and philanthropy, 63–66
    state budget deficits and, 13, 84–86
Fox, Maddy, 100–102
Framework for Providing All Students
    an Opportunity to Learn through
    Reauthorization of the Elementary and
    Secondary Education Act, 117–118
Franchises, 22
Frankenberg, E., 38
Freedom Schools, 33
Free market charters, 21, 26–28, 57, 68–84,
    113–114
Freudenberg, N., 105
Fruchter, N., 58
Fryer, R. G., Jr., 38, 39
Fuller, Ed, 49
Funding for schools
    call for investment, 117–125
    charter schools, 14, 43
    corruption in, 30–31
    decline in federal, 120–121
    Innovation Fund, 23
    per/capita/per-child, 28–33
    philanthropic/hedge-fund movement,
        19–20, 63–66
    prison expenditures versus, 13
    public-private combinations, 29–30
    Race to the Top initiative. *See* Race to
        the Top
    state budget deficits and, 13, 84–86,
        108–111, 121–122

Gabriel, Trip, 63
Gap, 65
Garcia, David R., 32, 38, 47
Gates, Bill, 31
Gates Foundation, 20, 29–30, 31, 63,
    64–65, 104
GEMS (Grassroots Education Movement),
    83
Georgia, 24
Gilder, Richard, 67
Gilder Foundation, 67
Gill, B., 38
Gintis, H., 88
Glass, G. V., 103
Glazer, Lee, 49–50
Gleason, P., 38, 40
Golden, D., 64
Goldsmith, S., 57
Gonzalez, Juan, 27, 31, 33–34, 76, 80, 81,
    98
Goodwin, Carter, 33
Graduation rates, 48–52
Grassroots Education in New York City, 127
Grassroots movements
    in California, 34–35
    in Chicago, 114, 115, 127
    in New Orleans, 35
    in New York City, 56–57, 126, 127
    in Philadelphia, 114, 116–117
    of teachers, 83, 127
Great Depression, 13–14
Green Dot network (California), 15, 22,
    34–35, 72
Grossman, A., 38
Grossman, K., 115
Gwynne, J., 38, 96, 97

Haney, Walter, 103
Hanushek, E., 38
Hargraves, William, 57
Harlem Children Zone (HCZ; New York
    City), 14–15, 29, 125–126
Harlem Success Academies (New York
    City), 27–28, 53, 57, 81
Harmony Schools (Texas), 49
Hartford, Connecticut, 71
Harvey, David, 26, 91, 108
Hass, N., 27–28
Hawaii, 24
Hayek, Friedrich, 26, 97

Hedge funds, 19–20, 63–66
Hedges, Christopher, 62
Henig, Jeffrey R., 25–26, 39, 52
Hess, Frederick, 65
Hickory Foundation, 67
Hirsch, L., 103
History of charters, 17–21
    history of educational choice, 7–8
    Obama initiatives, 21. See also Race to
        the Top
    philanthropic/hedge-fund movement,
        19–20, 63–66
    as progressive, experimental
        alternatives, 18–19
    vouchers, 7, 17–18, 111
Hollenbeck, K., 42
Hoover Institute, 42
Housing market, 12–14, 77–78, 126
Hoxby, C. M., 38
Hu, W., 14
Huerta, Dolores, 22
Hurricane Katrina, 91–95, 105–106
Hursh, D., 39, 95–97
Hurston, Zora Neale, 33
Huzienga, J. C., 66

Icahn, Carl, 67
Illinois. See Chicago
Imagine Network, 70, 71–72
Immigrant students, 44–45, 127
India, 13
Inner City Struggle and Community
    Coalition (Los Angeles), 127
Innovation. See also Charter schools/
    charter-school movement
    branding charters as innovative, 80–81
    hypothesis of innovation-contagion,
        54–55
    ignoring public sector, 83–84
    promise-evidence gap, 39, 53–57
    teacher experience and stability in,
        57–59
Innovation Fund, 23
Institute on Race and Policy, 94
Institute on Race and Poverty, 38, 46, 94

Jackson, Camille, 38, 47
Japan, 13
Jensen, N., 38
Jim Crow segregation, 33

K–12, 21, 77
Kahlenberg, R., 38
Kain, J., 38
Kang, J., 38
Kansas, 24, 44–45, 71
Karp, S., 88–89, 103
Keeton, A., 103
Kim, H., 38
Kinoy, A., 7, 88–89
Kiona, Ana, 46–47
KIPP (Knowledge is Power), 15–16, 22, 49, 58–59, 72
Kisida, B., 38
Klein, Joel, 42, 53, 57, 77
Klein, Naomi, 11, 89, 108
Klinsky, Steven, 74
Knowledge is Power (KIPP), 15–16, 22, 49, 58–59, 72
Knowles, T., 16, 38, 39, 49, 53–54
Kolodner, M., 31
Kovner, Bruce, 67
Kovner Foundation, 67
Kozol, J., 88
Krugman, Paul, 108
Kunnan, A. J., 38

Ladd, H., 38
*Land of Charters*, 85–86
Lapsey, Daniel, 38, 49
Lareau, Annette, 52
Latinos, equity and, 45–46
Lawyers Committee for Civil Rights Under the Law, 3–4, 38, 118–119
Leasing arrangements, 75–76
Lee, C., 38
Lee, K., 55
Lewis, Karen, 97–98
Libby, K., 72–74
Lindquist, Ben, 43
Lipman, Pauline, 28, 35, 39, 88–89, 95–97
Little Village/Lawndale High School (Chicago), 114, 115
Lobis, Joan, 99–100
Lotteries, 20, 40–41
Louisiana. *See* New Orleans
Lowell, James Russell, 88, 94, 99–100

Mack, J., 38
Madaus, George, 103
Magnet schools, 7

Manhattan Institute, 66
Manheimer, Virginia, 67
Marable, Manning, 108
Marketplace and charters, 21, 26–27. *See also* Privatization
　charter school entrepreneurs, 27–28, 57, 113–114
　market share, 77–84
　philanthropic/hedge fund movement, 19–20, 63–66
　profiting from privatization process, 21, 68–77
Marshall, A., 71
Maryland, 23, 71
Massachusetts, 24, 45
Mathematica Policy Research, 40–41, 43
Mathews, Jay, 84
Maxwell, L., 40
McCarthy era, 6
McEwan, Patrick, 55
McGee, J., 38
McGray, D., 15
McKinsey Consultants, 63
Medina, Jennifer, 8–9, 56, 63, 99, 104, 123
Mediratta, K., 100–101
Meeks, Gregory, 73–74
Meier, D., ix–xii, 7, 19, 24, 88–89
Merrick Academy Charter School (Queens Village, New York), 74
Michigan, 23, 24, 46, 71
　promise-evidence gap, 42, 55
　traditional schools versus charter schools, 55
Mickelson, R., 38
Miner, B., 18–19, 38, 39, 41
Minnesota, 18–19, 23, 46, 71
Miron, Gary, 17, 25, 32, 33, 49, 72–73, 124–125
Mishel, L., 38, 47
Mississippi, 127
Missouri, 44–45
Molnar, Alex, 24, 32, 70–71
"Mom and Pop" charters, 22
Monahan, R., 99
Morison, K., 104
Morris, Jerome E., 90, 105–106
Moscowitz, Eva, 27–28, 57
Moses, R., 88–89
Mulgrew, Michael, 32–33
*Mulgrew v. Board of Education*, 99

Muraka, S., 38

Nathan, Joe, 18
National Alliance for Public Charter
    Schools, 25
National Assessment of Educational
    Progress (NAEP), 122
National Board on Educational Testing and
    Public Policy, 103
National Commission on Excellence in
    Education, 12–13
National Council of Churches Governing
    Board, 117
National Heritage Academies Incorporated,
    66
*Nation at Risk*, 12–13
"Nations Best Charter Schools," 29
Neill, Monty, 84
Nevada, 71
Newark, New Jersey
    charter movement in, 110
    as educational petri dish, 48
    funding by Facebook founder, 30, 84
    hypothesis of innovation-contagion,
        54–55
    North Star Academy, 16, 44, 125–126
    promise-evidence gap and, 41
New Deal, 3
New Democrats, 3
New Jersey, 3, 23, 84, 110. *See also* Newark,
    New Jersey
    Abbott schools, 121–122
    budget crisis and public education,
        108–111, 121–122
    charter movement in, 51–52, 78–79,
        110–111, 123, 125
    poorest of the poor and, 47–48
New Markets Tax Credit, 76
New Mexico, 24
New Orleans, 35
    post-Katrina educational reforms, 91–
        95, 105–106
    promise-evidence gap and, 41
New Schools Venture Fund, 63
New York City
    charter-public school co-location, 56–57
    Coalition of Educational Justice, 127
    dropout/pushout/discharge rates,
        101–102
    educational management organizations

(EMOs), 73–74
Harlem Children Zone (HCZ), 14–15,
    29, 125–126
Harlem Success Academies, 27–28, 53,
    57, 81
labor-community partnership in, 83
Merrick Academy Charter School
    (Queens Village), 74
New York Flex Charter School, 77
parent engagement in, 53
PAVE charter school (Brooklyn), 76
Peninsula Preparatory Academy Charter
    School (Far Rockaway), 73–74
poorest of the poor in, 47
promise-evidence gap, 42, 44–48
school-choice campaign in Harlem
    (2008), 20
school closings/charter openings, 98–
    100, 101–102, 105–107
South Bronx Charter School for
    International Culture and the Arts, 74
testing fraud, 42
New York Collective of Radical Educators
    (NYCORE), 83, 127
New York Flex Charter School (New York
    City), 77
New York Performance Standards, 84
New York state, 23
    charter campaign and political
        mobilization of private sector, 66–67
    charter school transparency
        requirements, 81, 123–125
    demands for charter school
        accountability, 81
    parent engagement in, 52–53
    teachers' unions, 32–33, 66–67, 74,
        123–125
    testing in, 103–104
New York State United Teachers (NYSUT),
    66–67, 74, 123–125
*New York Times, The*, 12, 13–14, 27, 63
Next Step PCS (Washington, D.C.), 22
Ni, Y., 55
Nichols-Barrer, B. I., 38
No Child Left Behind (NCLB), 13, 126–127
North Carolina, 44–45
North Star Academy (Newark), 16, 44,
    125–126
NYCORE (New York Collective of Radical
    Educators), 83, 127

Oakes, Jeannie, 52
Obama, Barack, 7, 12, 14, 15, 21, 41,
    63–65, 86
O'Donnell, Daniel, 53
Ohio, 22, 25
    Cleveland Academy of Math, Science
        and Technology, 48
    Legislative Office of Education
        Oversight (LOEO), 42
    promise-evidence gap, 42, 44
Ohlin Foundation, 20
Oppositional approach, 79–84
    branding charters as innovative, 80–81
    demonizing teachers and unions, 82–83
    discrediting public education, 2, 3–4,
        80–81
    ignoring public sector innovation, 83–84
    private sector in education, 19–20,
        63–66
Orfield, Gary, 7, 45, 46
Otterman, S., 38, 52–53, 98, 99

Padres y Jóvenes Unidos (Denver), 127
Pappas, L., 103
Parent engagement
    effect of charters on, 52–53
    Folk Arts-Cultural Treasures Charter
        School (Philadelphia), 22, 114,
        116–117
    grassroots efforts, 114–117, 127
    Little Village/Lawndale High School
        (Chicago), 114, 115
    promise-evidence gap, 39, 52–53
    public accountability and, 85–86
    search for alternatives, 33–36
Parent Union (California), 34–35
Paterson, David, 66
PAVE charter school (Brooklyn, New York),
    76
Payne, Charles M., 16, 38, 39, 49, 53–54,
    88–89
PDK/Gallup Poll, 2–3
Peninsula Preparatory Academy Charter
    School (Far Rockaway, New York),
    73–74
Pennsylvania, 71. *See also* Philadelphia
Perkins, B., 8–9
Perkins, T., 7, 88–89
Peterson, B., 18–19, 38, 39, 41
Petrilli, Mike, 44

Phi Delta Kappan, 2–3, 84
Philadelphia
    Folk Arts-Cultural Treasures Charter
        School, 22, 114, 116–117
    transition to charter schools, 58
Philanthropic/hedge-fund movement,
    19–20, 63–66
Pickett, Kate, 90, 119
Placencia, Perla, 45–46
Policy
    accountability of charters, 25–26
    authorization of charters, 23
    autonomy of charters, 24
    charter schools as public institutions,
        23–26
    impact of dispossession, 100–102
    influence of wealth on, 62–63
    length of charter contract, 24
    state and philanthropy, 63–66
    statewide caps on development of
        charters, 25, 43–45, 81, 123
    strategic organization of charter
        campaign, 77–84
    types of charter schools, 21–23, 69–70
Policy Matters Ohio, 70
Polling for Justice (PFJ), 100–101
Poverty
    equity and, 47–48
    inequality and "crisis" of education,
        90–91
Powell, J., 38
Prison expenditures, 13
Privatization, 61–87
    consolidation of power and, 69–75
    economic gain from, 68–77
    influence of wealth on public policy,
        62–63
    loss of accountability, 84–86
    market share and, 77–84
    in New York State, 66–67
    in post-Katrina New Orleans, 92–94,
        105–106
    state and philanthropy, 63–66
Program for International Student
    Assessment (PISA), 12–13
Progressive educational reform, 2, 7, 54,
    127–128
Promise-evidence gap, 37–60
    dropouts/pushouts/graduation rates,
        48–52

Promise-evidence gap, *continued*
    equity, 38, 45–48
    experience, quality, and retention of
        educators, 39, 57–59
    innovation, 39, 53–57
    national versus local evidence, 41–42
    parent engagement, 39, 52–53
    summary of evidence on, 59–60
    test-score achievement data, 37–41,
        43–45, 55
Public education
    binary tradeoffs of charter policy, 109,
        111–114
    co-location of charter schools in public
        schools, 8–9, 56–57
    critique of, 2, 3–4
    discrediting, 2, 3–4, 80–81
    ignoring public sector innovation,
        83–84
    impact of charters on traditional
        schools, 55, 59–60
    New Jersey budget crisis, 108–111
    privatization of public schools, 68,
        75–77
    profit and consolidation of power,
        69–75
    profiting from privatization of public
        schools, 68–77
    reimagining/reinvesting in, 125–129
    state and philanthropy, 63–66
    wealth and public policy, 62–63
Pushout rates, 48–52, 101–102, 104–105

Race to the Top, 3–4, 7, 13–14, 21, 23, 86,
        118, 126–127
    demonization of teachers, 82
    funds aligned with advocacy objectives,
        81
    lift of state caps, 25, 43–45, 81, 123
Ramsey, Nadine, 92–93
Ravitch, Diane, 21, 38, 42, 62–64
Raymond, Margaret, 42
Reagan, Ronald, 62, 121
Real estate interests, 12–14, 70, 73–78, 126
Reardon, S. F., 38
Recovery School District (New Orleans),
        92–93
Reich, R., 78
Renaissance 2010 plan (Chicago), 95–98,
        102, 105–107

Renzulli, L., 38, 47
Rethinking Schools, 127
Ritter, G., 38
Rivkin, S., 38
Robelen, Eric W., 38, 49
Robert W. Wilson Trust, 67
Robin Hood foundation, 29
Roda, A., 47
Rogers, Margot, 64
Rogosa, D., 38, 42
Roy, J., 38, 47
Ruglis, J., 90, 91, 100–105
Rutgers University, National Education
        Policy Center, 47–48

Sadovnik, A. R., 38, 39, 41, 103
Salah, S., 100–101
Sass, T., 38
Sattin-Bajaj, C., 38
Schemo, D., 37–40
School Choice Scholarships, 67
Schoolhouse Finance, 70
Schundler, Brett, 110
SEED schools, 49–50
Shanker, Albert, 2, 18, 19
Shelton, James, 64
Silver, Sheldon, 81
Singapore, 121
Slovacek, S. P., 38
Smarick, Andy, 78–79
Smith, Malcolm, 73–74
Smith, J., 35
Smith, T., 39
Socialization process, 6
Social justice, 18–19
Social stratification, 46–47, 90–91, 94–95
South Bronx Charter School for
        International Culture and the Arts
        (New York City), 74
Southern Echo (Mississippi), 127
Southworth, S., 38
Spellings, Margaret, 93–94
Spoto, M. A., 110
SRI International, 49
Stand-alone charters, 70
Stanford University, Center for Research
        on Education Outcomes (CREDO), 10,
        25, 38–41, 43, 73
Stoudt, B., 100–102
Strickland, C., 88–89

Student achievement. *See also* Testing
  test-score achievement data, 37–41,
    43–45
  U.S. versus other countries, 12–13,
    120–121
Students at the Center, 92
Students in special education, 45–46, 113
Stuit, D., 39
Success Charter Network lottery, 20
Surrey, D., 7, 88–89

Tanner, R. A., 88–89
Tashlik, P., 19, 24, 54, 88–89, 104–105
Teachers
  current job market, 14
  demonization of, 82–83
  grassroots efforts, 83, 127
  promise-evidence gap, 39, 57–59
  Teach for America (TFA), 58
Teachers' unions, 2, 28, 30, 32–33, 82–85,
    97–99, 110, 122–124, 128–129
Teach for America (TFA), 58
*Teaching Tolerance* (Jackson), 47
Tea Party, 126
Tenure systems, 82
Testing
  charter schools and, 7–8, 27, 55, 83–84
  dispossession impact of, 102–104
  exit exams, 103–104
  international, 12–13, 120–121
  New York City fraud, 42
  promise-evidence gap, 37–41, 43–45, 55
  racial impact of, 103–104
  Renaissance 2010 plan (Chicago), 96
Texas, 71
  Harmony Schools, 49
  promise-evidence gap, 42, 55
  testing in, 103
  traditional schools versus charter
    schools, 33
  Yes Prep (Houston), 58, 72
Texas Center for Educational Research, 42
Think tanks, 20
Thomas B. Fordham Institute, 28–29, 44
Toch, Tom, 16, 29, 43–44, 58, 65–66
Toppo, G., 49
Trends in International Mathematics and
    Science Study (TIMSS), 12–13
Trenton, New Jersey, 110
*Turnaround Challenge, The*, 65

Tuttle, C., 38, 40
Uncommon Ground, 15–16
Uncommon Schools, 72
United Federation of Teachers, 32–33, 99
U.S. Department of Education, 40, 57, 64,
    101
University of California at Los Angeles
    (UCLA), Civil Rights Project, 46
University of Chicago Charter Schools, 16
Urban Youth Collaborative, 127
Urschel, J., 72, 124–125
*USA Today*, 49

Valenzuela, Angela, 52, 103
Van Lier, P., 70–72
Victory Schools Inc., 31, 74
Visconti, L., 38, 39, 41
Vouchers, 7, 17–18, 111

*Waiting for Superman* (film), 3, 49–50, 113
Walker, V. S., 33, 88–89
Wal-Mart, 66–67
Walters, S., 18–19, 38, 39, 41
Walton, John, 66
Walton Family Foundation, 20, 29–30, 64,
    65, 66–67
Washington, D.C., 22, 24, 25, 30
  SEED school, 49–50
Washington Post, 84
Weiher, G. R., 39, 55
Wells, Amy Stuart, 38, 39, 41, 47, 111
Western New York Maritime Charter
    Schools, 67
White Hat Management, 21, 71, 72
Wilkinson, Richard, 90, 119
Winfrey, Oprah, 84
Wisconsin, 23
Wolff, Daniel, 75
Woodson, C., 88–89
Wright, Keith, 57
Wyoming, 24

Yes Prep (Houston), 58, 72

Zelon, H., 15, 77
Zhao, Yong, 12–13, 103
Zimmer, R., 38, 39, 55
Zones of dispossession, 101
Zuckerberg, Mark, 30

# About the Authors

**Michael Fabricant** is a professor at the Hunter College School of Social Work and executive officer of the Ph.D. Program in Social Welfare. He has published on the political economy of the welfare state, homelessness, settlement houses, community organizing, the fiscal crisis of nonprofit agencies, and public education policy. For the past 6 years he has been a principal officer of the Professional Staff Congress of the City University of New York, a union of 22,000 faculty and staff. Equally important, he has been a community leader and advocate on questions of housing and homelessness. Dr. Fabricant has founded four nonprofits in the state of New Jersey and served on their boards. For 10 years he was a board member and principal officer of the National Coalition for the Homeless. He is the author of seven books and numerous articles. His most recent books include *Settlement Houses Under Siege: The Struggle to Sustain Community Organizations in New York City* (Columbia University Press, 2002) and *Organizing for Educational Justice: The Campaign for School Reform in the South Bronx* (University of Minnesota Press, 2010). He is presently working with Michelle Fine on *The Twilight of American Empire and the Colonization of Public Education* (Paradigm Publishers, 2012).

**Michelle Fine** is a distinguished professor of Social Psychology, Women's Studies, and Urban Education at the Graduate Center, CUNY, and is a founding faculty member of the Public Science Project (PSP). A consortium of researchers, policy makers, and community activists, PSP produces critical scholarship "to be of use" in social policy debates and organizing movements for educational equity and human rights. Recent books and policy monographs include *Revolutionizing Education: Youth Participatory Action Research in Motion* (with Julio Cammarota, Routledge, 2008); *Muslim-American Youth* (with Selcuk Sirin, New York University Press, 2008); and "Changing minds: The impact of college on women in prison," which is nationally recognized as the primary empirical basis for the contemporary college in prison movement (2001), and is best known for *Framing Dropouts* (SUNY, 1991). Additionally, Fine has provided expert testimony in a number of ground-breaking legal victories, including women's access to the Citadel Military Academy and in *Williams v. California,* a class action lawsuit for urban youth-of-color denied adequate education in California. Fine is the recipient of the 2011 Kurt Lewin Award from the Society for the Psychological Study of Social Issues and the 2010 Social Justice and Higher Education Award from the College and Community Fellowship.